REMAIN

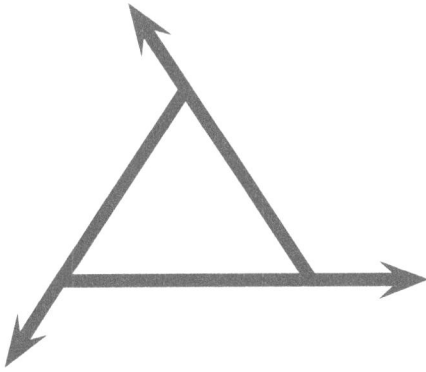

JACOB PHELPS

LUCIDBOOKS

To my beautiful wife: Angie, you are a living example of God's love and grace. You will forever be more than I deserve, and I cherish each moment we are together.

To my fearless daughter: Ellie, you are one of the most compassionate individuals I have ever known. I pray each day that you will continue to learn what it means to care for those who have been rejected by this world. Be kind and loving.

To my gentle son: Brecken, your passion and drive to protect and defend the weak are traits not often seen in this world. Jesus laid down his life for others, and I pray you continue to do the same. Be strong and courageous.

Contents

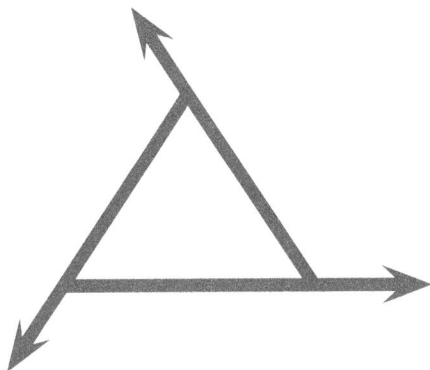

Introduction

O bedience is the call of every disciple. If we truly love Jesus, we will do what he says. Real obedience rises from devotion, reverence, and adoration reserved only for the one thing that has taken hold of our hearts, so when claiming to follow Jesus, we're making a staunch declaration that frames our words, thoughts, and actions. We should take seriously the command to go and make disciples:

If you love me, you will keep my commandments. And I will ask the Father, and he will give you another Helper, to be with you forever, even the Spirit of truth, whom the world cannot receive, because it neither sees him nor knows him. You know him, for he dwells with you and will be in you. I will not leave you as orphans; I will come to you. Yet a little while and the world will see me no more, but you will see me. Because I live, you also will live. In that day you will know that I am in my Father, and you in me, and I in you. Whoever has my commandments and keeps them, he it is who loves me. And he who loves me will be loved by my Father, and I will love him and manifest myself to him.

—John 14:15–21

And being found in human form, he humbled himself by becoming obedient to the point of death, even death on a cross.

—Philippians 2:8

The problem is that most of the time in churches we haven't really shown anyone how to make disciples. At best, we've taught people to be spiritually educated and morally minded, but to many, Jesus's example of "obedient unto death" is just a story instead of a master plan for living. Participation in a local congregation has become the sign of a true believer. We think the more events people attend, the better they must be. Being present at worship services, small groups, camps, and mission trips have become the sought-after standard instead of living in obedience to imitate Jesus. We might say churches emphasize both, but an extreme focus on one will undoubtedly diminish the other while focusing on the correct one will elevate all things pertaining to our worship of God.

Making disciples is hard. Jesus dedicated his life to twelve men, teaching them to do the same with those they would disciple in the future. His last words to them were a reminder of his expectations and their true purpose in life. It was their responsibility to teach people to obey everything he had commanded, and that responsibility is passed on to future believers.

In other words, if we are not busy making disciples, we are being disobedient. On a personal level, I had to confront this reality in my own life. I was a moral person, preaching the Word of God, but I wasn't actually making disciples. All my efforts were going into preparing sermons instead of preparing people to make disciples of their own. I'm convinced we must rediscover what it means to be a disciple who makes disciples, and that's what this book is about. My prayer is that you would be open to confronting some uncomfortable things in your own life and finding real joy in God's call to obedience.

PART ONE
THE IMAGO DEI

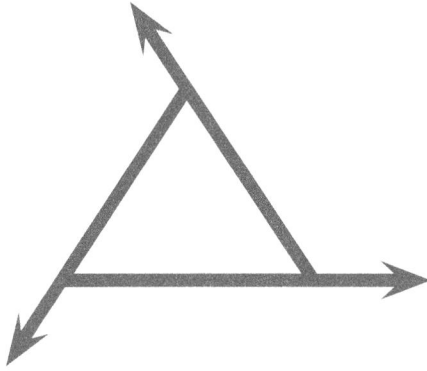

The Imago Dei in Scripture

How God created us and for what purpose is clear in Scripture. As individuals, we were not created for different reasons in the grand scheme of eternity. All of humanity was brought into existence for the glory of God, so studying the creation of man and woman is paramount in our understanding of disciple-making and God's intention for our lives. It all starts with the Imago Dei.

Where do I find the Imago Dei?

The Imago Dei is first found in Genesis, chapter one. From the very beginning, we can see God intended a special relationship with humanity. Nothing else would compare to his prized creation.

> Then God said, "Let us make man in our image, after our likeness. And let them have dominion over the fish of

the sea and over the birds of the heavens and over the livestock and over all the earth and over every creeping thing that creeps on the earth." So God created man in his own image, in the image of God he created him; male and female he created them. And God blessed them. And God said to them, "Be fruitful and multiply and fill the earth and subdue it, and have dominion over the fish of the sea and over the birds of the heavens and over every living thing that moves on the earth."

—Genesis 1:26–28

Unfortunately, Christians have mostly seen these verses as nothing more than proof that God made them special, uniquely set apart from the rest of creation. While true, the importance of the image of God in every human being goes far deeper. A problem arises when we read Scripture as a series of loosely interconnected stories instead of one big story. In other words, we don't get a full picture of what the Imago Dei represents unless we look at it from a holistic standpoint. In their book, *The Drama of Scripture*, Craig Bartholomew, and Michael Goheen make a powerful argument regarding a complete approach to the Word of God instead of the fragmented one we usually get in churches today:

The Christian too believes that there is one true story: the story told in the Bible. It begins with God's creation and human rebellion and runs through the history of Israel to Jesus and on through the church, moving to the coming of the kingdom of God. At the very center of this story is the man called Jesus in whom God has revealed his fullest purpose and meaning for the world. Only in this one narrative can we discover the meaning of human history—and thus the meaning of your life and mine.

This kind of story is basic and foundational. It provides us with an understanding of the whole world and of our own place within it. Such a comprehensive story gives us the meaning of not merely personal or national history but universal history.[1]

In other words, if the meaning of our lives is somehow wrapped up in the Imago Dei (which we believe to be true), we should discover what it means in Scripture and allow the Holy Spirit to restore what sin has tainted. I believe the Bible is very precise and definitive when it comes to the Image of God. Bill Clem rightly draws attention to the way sin distorts the Imago Dei.

> The image of God is a quality, a characteristic, an attribute, a function, and a relational capacity that allows a human to image God in a way that pleases and glorifies him. The Bible is not precise or definitive as to what the image of God is, yet God is clear in his Word that every human is an image bearer. The capacity to bear his image in some distorted way survived the sinful fall of mankind.[2]

While Clem accurately states the devastating effect of sin in our lives, he's wrong in his assertion about the Bible's lack of clarity with the Imago Dei. Reading the Imago Dei passage in

---

1 Craig G. Bartholomew and Michael W. Goheen, *The Drama of Scripture: Finding Our Place in the Biblical Story* (Grand Rapids, MI: Baker Academic, 2014), 20.

2 Bill Clem, *Disciple: Getting Your Identity from Jesus* (Wheaton, IL: Crossway, 2011), 60.

light of the entirety of Scripture should give us a fuller picture of what God meant when he created humans in his image. Genesis 1:26–28 contains the fullness of the idea of the Imago Dei, but additional details and clarity came later through a different person, also inspired by God.

Peter elaborates on this reality. He understood all of time as a testament to God's plan. Until Jesus walked this earth, not even prophets of old were able to fully comprehend the lengths God would go to restore his creation.

> Concerning this salvation, the prophets who prophesied about the grace that was to be yours searched and inquired carefully, inquiring what person or time the Spirit of Christ in them was indicating when he predicted the sufferings of Christ and the subsequent glories. It was revealed to them that they were serving not themselves but you, in the things that have now been announced to you through those who preached the good news to you by the Holy Spirit sent from heaven, things into which angels long to look.
>
> —1 Peter 1:10–12

Knowing this, we can freely and confidently look at all of Scripture and gather an in-depth knowledge of the Imago Dei. Only then can we get a clear picture of what we should strive for as followers of Jesus. Scripture is the key.

What Is the Imago Dei?

The Imago Dei exists in every human being who has ever lived. If anything, Genesis 1:26 makes it very clear who humans are patterned after. The standard is the perfection found in God. Let us take one more look at this passage.

Obviously, God remains the main character here (a reality we would be smart to remember for the rest of our lives), but surely the Image of God is in reference to more than just a mere similarity to the physical nature of God. Other references to God's physical appearance in Scripture, which are sometimes extremely nonhuman-like, should quickly dispel such a shallow view of the Imago Dei. God created humanity with more than a physical aesthetic in mind. He has a purpose for everything, and that purpose is evident from the beginning. If we are made in the image of God, then we can look to him as a blueprint for our own existence. This doesn't mean we get to be a god or even god-like. Those are attributes God refuses to share with his creation, but it does mean that our best existence is only found when we mirror the image in which we were created.

From a scriptural standpoint, all of this points to Jesus, the perfect reflection of his Heavenly Father. Remember, Jesus told us, "My Father, who has given them to me, is greater than all, and no one is able to snatch them out of the Father's hand. I and the Father are one" (John 10:29–30). Paul goes on to explain things further in his letter to the church in Colossae:

> He is the image of the invisible God, the firstborn of all creation. For by him all things were created, in heaven and on earth, visible and invisible, whether thrones or dominions or rulers or authorities—all things were created through him and for him. And he is the head of the body, the church. He is the beginning, the firstborn from the dead, that in everything he might be preeminent. For in him all the fullness of God was pleased to dwell, and through him to reconcile to himself all things, whether on earth or in heaven, making peace by the blood of his cross.
>
> —Colossians 1:15–20

Two things should be pointed out in this passage specifically dealing with the topic at hand. First, Paul claims Jesus is the visible image of the invisible God, meaning he shares the same substance as God and gives us a complete view of God's character that we can understand and comprehend. This means that if we are made in the image of God, we're made to reflect and mirror the glory we see in Jesus, including every attribute and desire given to him by his Father. We should strive to imitate his words, thoughts, and deeds. Everything Jesus did on this earth is a blueprint for those who follow him. Paul reinforced this idea when he said, "Be imitators of me, as I am of Christ" (1 Corinthians 11:1).

Second, while the reconciliation Paul speaks of surely includes all of creation, within that we find the reconciliation of humanity and the Imago Dei. For those whom God has called and who freely choose to follow him, salvation happens immediately, but the restoration of the Imago Dei is a lifelong process. The image of God can be fully seen and understood in Jesus. He is the blueprint for the Imago Dei.

Sin Distorts the Imago Dei

When sin entered the world through Adam, everything self-destructed. Paul tells us, "Therefore, just as sin came into the world through one man, and death through sin, and so death spread to all men because all sinned" (Romans 5:12). Everything is broken because of sin. Nothing is how it was created to be, and that includes the Imago Dei found in every man and woman. In Ephesians, Paul explains the devastation of sin and how it affects our life pursuits:

> And you were dead in the trespasses and sins in which you once walked, following the course of this world, following

the prince of the power of the air, the spirit that is now at work in the sons of disobedience—among whom we all once lived in the passions of our flesh, carrying out the desires of the body and the mind, and were by nature children of wrath, like the rest of mankind.

—Ephesians 2:1–3

In essence, if Jesus is the blueprint for the Imago Dei, then we are broken to the point where we no longer resemble anything like our Heavenly Father. The image of God in us is distorted. We don't mirror the attributes of Christ.

Imagine a row of funhouse mirrors. One might make you look taller than you ever will be, and another will make you seem wider than you ever want to be. Others may distort your image to the point that nothing in the reflection is recognizable. Sin has effectively made us a funhouse mirror that no longer accurately represents the Imago Dei.

Jesus came to die on the cross so sin would no longer have power over our lives. Paul proclaims, "For our sake he made him to be sin who knew no sin, so that in him we might become the righteousness of God" (2 Corinthians 5:21). Our own righteousness could never come close to resembling the righteousness of God. Peter says it like this:

He committed no sin, neither was deceit found in his mouth. When he was reviled, he did not revile in return; when he suffered, he did not threaten, but continued entrusting himself to him who judges justly. He himself bore our sins in his body on the tree, that we might die to sin and live to righteousness. By his wounds you have been healed.

—1 Peter 2:22–24

Sin may no longer have power over those who have chosen to follow Jesus, but the wounds it leaves are deep and long-lasting. Paul understood the struggle of sin and how it affects our ability to live for Jesus. In his letter to the church in Corinth, he encourages those caught in their own sin, "Wake up from your drunken stupor, as is right, and do not go on sinning" (1 Corinthians 15:34). The Holy Spirit will not fix the distorted image of God in our lives while we struggle with unrepentant behavior.

Restoring the Imago Dei

If sin taints and distorts the image of God in all humans, the work of the Holy Spirit is the only thing capable of restoring God's image in us. We want restoration to be an instantaneous thing, but that would deny the power and seriousness of sin. In reality, allowing the Holy Spirit to change us so we can properly reflect Christ is something we'll be working on for the rest of our lives. It's hard work. Thankfully, we're not alone in our efforts. Paul tells us, "For those whom he foreknew he also predestined to be conformed to the image of his Son, in order that he might be the firstborn among many brothers" (Romans 8:29). We were never meant to stay in sin. Sin mangles, but God restores.

The Imago Dei is the target. Jesus is the blueprint for the image of God, and he is our prize when this life is over. What sin takes away from us is nothing compared to what God has in store for those who follow him. Paul wrote to the church in Corinth, "Just as we have borne the image of the man of dust, we shall also bear the image of the man of heaven" (1 Corinthians 15:49). That image is still inside us at the moment, but it's perverted and defiled by our own sin.

We must take responsibility for not living up to God's

purpose for our lives, but in his grace and mercy, he allows us to chase after and attain that purpose with the help of the Holy Spirit. It's a lifelong transformation taking place daily. Paul states, "And we all, with unveiled face, beholding the glory of the Lord, are being transformed into the same image from one degree of glory to another. For this comes from the Lord who is the Spirit" (2 Corinthians 3:18). The Imago Dei is the goal of every true disciple.

The Imago Dei and Disciple-Making

When it comes to making disciples, a program or Bible study hour will never fully do the trick. Teaching people to hear and obey the things of God is more than passing on information from one vessel to another. From Scripture, we know that discipleship requires far more than most people are willing to give, but the payoff is something greater than we could ever hope or imagine. Education is only one part of what it means to make disciples. Jesus verbally taught his disciples all the time, but he was also the master of modeling and contextualization. Everything he said, did and thought had an end goal in mind. His disciple-making method was his life, lived for all to see. Even in his most intimate moments, such as in the Garden of Gethsemane, Jesus showed his closest disciples what it meant to live in obedience.

He molded his disciples to look, act, think, and speak with a distinct purpose in mind. That doesn't mean individuals were robbed of their personalities and gifts in order to manufacture mindless clones, but it does mean those gifts and human intricacies were trained to chase after one unifying purpose: to fill the earth with God-worshiping image-bearers.

Genesis 1:27–28 reminds us that God plans to fill the earth with image-bearers who will worship and obey him forever.

When sin entered the world, it twisted all of creation into an improper and undeserved worship of other things. Mark Liederbach, one of my doctoral professors, used the illustration of a compass to explain what has happened to the worship of people in this world and the misdirection of their lives.

In this scenario, God is represented by the idea of "True North."[3] In other words, he never changes. He created everything exactly the way he wanted it to be, and that includes the purpose for existence. Remember, we've learned that Jesus is the blueprint for the Imago Dei. He is both God and the perfect representation of God in human form. That's where we get the whole scenario of "100 percent God, 100 percent man" in doctrinal form. He is God, but because he humbled himself in human form, Jesus is now the focus of our imitation. His example is how we know what the image of God looks like in flesh.

Humanity's true purpose, which is to perfectly worship and obey God forever (which Jesus did), can be seen in the shorter arrow above. We were made to chase after God's glory for an eternity, but sin twisted everything. It messed up the image of God inside us.

3 Mark Liederbach and Seth Bible, *True North: Christ, the Gospel, and Creation Care* (Nashville, TN: B & H Academic, 2012), 8.

We can represent what sin does to our lives by moving the arrow away from true north. As you can see, sin has completely distorted our worship of God and our ability to perfectly reflect the Imago Dei.

We don't come close to looking like Jesus because we worship things that don't matter. The goal of disciple-making is reordering or reverting that worship back to its original object of affection. Allowing the Holy Spirit to change us from the inside out takes time. Truthfully, it's a process that will continue our entire lives. Disciple-making is course correction. The more we learn to live, love, think, and speak like Jesus, the more we reflect the true image of God.

Scripturally speaking, God has designed three things as necessary for the restoration of the Imago Dei. First, we need the work of the Holy Spirit in our lives. Second, we have to work hard at becoming a disciple ourselves. We need spiritual disciplines, or habits, which are avenues for the Holy Spirit to actually change us. Finally, we need a disciple, someone who is going to teach us what it means to follow Christ. We require the "withness" of other people.

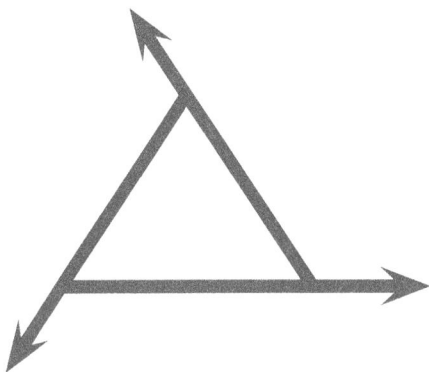

CHAPTER TWO

Restoration of the Imago Dei

Is It Really That Simple?

J esus is the blueprint for the Imago Dei. To restore the image of God in us, we must learn to imitate Christ. As simple as that may sound, accomplishing such a feat is impossible on our own. In fact, the difficulty of such an endeavor frustrates and stalemates Christians every day. Thankfully, God has provided a clear path for our restoration.

If Jesus is the standard for living a life that reflects God in his fullness, there must be a way to fix what is broken in our lives. Salvation is immediate, but the mending of sin's devastating effects takes a lifetime. I speak to people all the time who are frustrated with their own lack of growth as followers of Christ. In most cases, they simply haven't put forth the effort required; they don't understand how the Holy Spirit works in their lives to change their current situation. They have made the decision to follow Jesus, but spend days, months, years, or decades waiting for God to do his job and change them through some miraculous, supernatural work.

As tempting as it sounds to sit back and let God do all the work while we bask in the glory of our salvation, we never see the Holy Spirit work that way in the Bible. If God has carefully planned the beginning and end of all things on earth, he has surely planned how his children grow and mature. Disciple-making requires three things: the power and work of the Holy Spirit, the diligent teaching and modeling from a disciple, and the pursuit of godliness from individual believers.

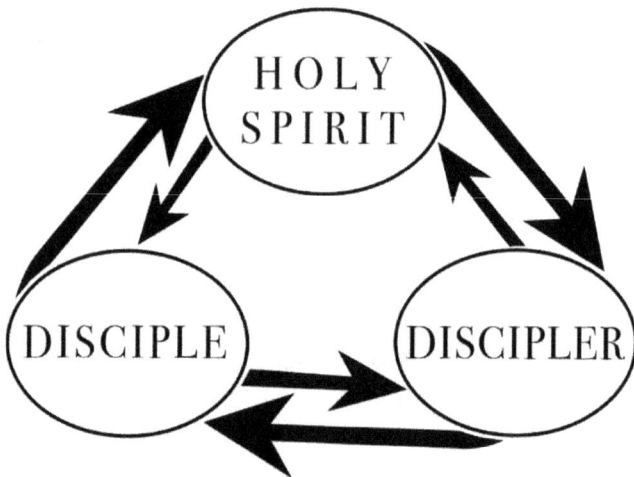

The Holy Spirit

Let's look at what Scripture says about the Holy Spirit. Jesus spoke of the Spirit to his disciples and explained what his job would be. His interaction with humanity has massive implications for the restoration of the Imago Dei in every believer.

When the Spirit of truth comes, he will guide you into all the truth, for he will not speak on his own authority, but whatever he hears he will speak, and he will declare to you the things that are to come.

—John 16:13

The Spirit *guides* us. Without him, religion quickly becomes about following rules for the sake of following rules. The Spirit leads and directs us to true life change. True life change means we look more like Jesus today than we did yesterday. This type of change leads to advancing the Kingdom of God. Only the Spirit knows the narrow path of righteousness.

He also *helps* us amid our own frailty. Sin has broken everything and left us vulnerable to a life of destruction. We need the Holy Spirit to do what we cannot do and be strong in our weaknesses. Paul speaks of this need in his letter to the church in Rome.

Likewise the Spirit helps us in our weakness. For we do not know what to pray for as we ought, but the Spirit himself intercedes for us with groanings too deep for words. And he who searches hearts knows what is the mind of the Spirit, because the Spirit intercedes for the saints according to the will of God.

—Romans 8:26–27

Everyone, at one time or another, has experienced a form of spiritual paralysis. The weight of sin and wickedness is so heavy that we become stuck. We're fully aware of our inability to move but can't express the pain we feel due to the effects of a sinful world. God does not want us to stay in this place of frustration. Far too often, the frustration leads to self-pity or, in more severe cases, deep depression. At times like this, the Holy Spirit intercedes on our behalf.

The Holy Spirit is God, the third person in the trinity, and a gift to all believers. Without the Spirit, there would be no heavenly revelation; there would be no hope. The Spirit *gives* us the mind of Christ. Read what Paul says in 1 Corinthians 2:6–16.

> Yet among the mature we do impart wisdom, although it is not the wisdom of this age or of the rulers of this age, who are doomed to pass away. But we impart a secret and hidden wisdom of God, which God decreed before the ages for our glory. None of the rulers of this age understood this, for if they had, they would not have crucified the Lord of glory. But, as it is written, "What no eye has seen, nor ear heard, nor the heart of man imagined, what God has prepared for those who love him"—these things God has revealed to us through the Spirit. For the Spirit searches everything, even the depths of God. For who knows a person's thoughts except for the spirit of that person, which is in him? So also no one comprehends the thoughts of God except the Spirit of God. Now we have received not the spirit of the world, but the Spirit who is from God, that we might understand the things freely given us by God. And we impart this in words not taught by human wisdom but taught by the Spirit, interpreting spiritual truths to those who are spiritual. The natural person does not accept the things of the Spirit of God, for they are folly to him, and he is not able to understand them because they are spiritually discerned. The spiritual person judges all things but is himself to be judged by no one. "For who has understood

the mind of the Lord so as to instruct him?" But we have the mind of Christ.

—1 Corinthians 2:6–16

We are only capable of understanding God's plan and purpose because the Holy Spirit makes it clear to us. In reality, our broken and sinful minds could never fathom the greatness of God or his plan for our lives. Without the help of the Holy Spirit in illuminating spiritual things, the Imago Dei would be a mystery, and good deeds of any kind would lose their meaning. Knowledge and moral living do not create spiritually mature believers. Plenty of people attend church their entire lives and know a lot about Jesus, but they don't resemble him at all. They're impressed with Jesus and his character, but they don't desire his lordship.

Finally, it is the Spirit's job to *grow and create* in us the things we could never accomplish on our own. These are known as the "fruit of the Spirit." They are the characteristics of God found perfectly mirrored in the Imago Dei. We find the epitome of each in Jesus.

But the fruit of the Spirit is love, joy, peace, patience, kindness, goodness, faithfulness, gentleness, self-control; against such things there is no law. And those who belong to Christ Jesus have crucified the flesh with its passions and desires. If we live by the Spirit, let us also keep in step with the Spirit.

—Galatians 5:16–25

We need the Holy Spirit to be disciples who make disciples. It's impossible to accomplish on our own, and the Holy Spirit doesn't work independently of humanity. He works in conjunction with believers. God doesn't need humanity, but he longs for his creation and passionately pursues us.

The Disciple and Spiritual Disciplines

Without the work of the Holy Spirit changing us from the inside out, spiritual disciplines become nothing more than a rigid form of piety, devoid of any purpose. However, combined with the transforming power of the Spirit, these disciplines are a focusing mechanism for true change. Doing things for the sake of doing things accomplishes nothing.

It's been said, "A sailor has no power over the wind, but a good sailor knows how to set his sail to the wind." This is why spiritual disciplines and passions matter. They are not an end goal, but they point to the end goal of godliness. Paul instructed Timothy on these things.

> Have nothing to do with irreverent, silly myths. Rather train yourself for godliness; for while bodily training is of some value, godliness is of value in every way, as it holds promise for the present life and also for the life to come.
>
> —1 Timothy 4:7–8

Spiritual disciplines combine with the power of the Holy Spirit to beget spiritual growth and maturity, but only if we allow the Holy Spirit to work in our lives. The separation of our own discipline from the work of the Spirit creates dysfunction. A few years ago, "What Would Jesus Do (WWJD)?" was a cultural phenomenon, if only because so many knew what it meant and what it was trying to accomplish. But it was destined to fail from the beginning. It was a reactionary question, and therefore, the wrong question. A more biblical question asks, "What did Jesus do?" If we're going to imitate Christ, then we have to understand how important it is to pursue our own spiritual formation. Jesus did it daily.

Spiritual formation is both an active pursuit of God and an allowance of the Holy Spirit to change our lives. Spiritual formation is achieved through spiritual disciplines, which are individual and corporate disciplines that encourage spiritual growth. We will look at two groups of spiritual disciplines: immediate and maturing. Immediate disciplines are those that new believers can quickly adopt. Maturing discipline often takes a little more time to master as new believers grow in their faith.

Spiritual disciplines are not the end goal. They are used to focus us. They are ways the Holy Spirit guides and changes us. As 1 Timothy 4:7 reminds us, we're training ourselves for godliness.

Immediate Spiritual Disciplines

Bible Study

All Scripture is breathed out by God and profitable for teaching, for reproof, for correction, and for training in righteousness, that the man of God may be complete, equipped for every good work.

—2 Timothy 3:16–17

All believers must study the Bible. Otherwise, we're trying to "wing it," which always leads to disastrous results. The Bible is God's revelation to us, but hearing a sermon once (or even twice) a week is not going to cut it. Jesus learned Scripture because he knew it was God's Word. Reading is one thing, but we can read and never be moved if we don't take the time to actually study what God tells us and put it into practice.

Prayer

> Watch and pray that you may not enter into temptation. The spirit indeed is willing, but the flesh is weak.
>
> —Matthew 26:41

We shouldn't pray because we're strong or super religious people. We pray because we're weak and need a really big God. Most of us struggle to pray for a few minutes, let alone an hour, but we find Jesus praying all the time in the Gospels. Jesus knew he needed to converse with his Father. We need to do so as well.

Worship

> I appeal to you therefore, brothers, by the mercies of God, to present your bodies as a living sacrifice, holy and acceptable to God, which is your spiritual worship.
>
> —Romans 12:1

Worship is a complete focus and response to God. We're responding to who he is and what he has done. If we're overwhelmed by his grace in our lives, then we will worship and obey. Believers need to worship corporately and individually. Their lives are to be an act of worship, and that means learning and doing the things God planned for them since the beginning of time.

Serving

> How much more will the blood of Christ, who through the eternal Spirit offered himself without blemish to God, purify our conscience from dead works to serve the living God.
>
> —Hebrews 9:14

Serving God is a privilege we often take for granted, but we need to serve him and his bride, the Church. He gifts us with talents, and more importantly, spiritual gifts with which to serve the Body of Christ. If you're not serving in the local church, then you are not pursuing one of the most important spiritual disciplines. The local church is one of the greatest ways to experience life in the Kingdom of God.

Maturing Spiritual Disciplines

Solitude

> Then Jesus was led up by the Spirit into the wilderness to be tempted by the devil.

> —Matthew 4:1

Most of us focus on the "to be tempted by the devil" part of the Scripture. What we miss is "Jesus was led up by the Spirit." There is something to be said about being alone and silent before God. Matthew 14:23, Mark 1:35, and Luke 4:42 are all times when Jesus sought alone time with God. We are constantly connected to something, and we need time when it's just us and God. This means no music or background noise to make things "less weird." Oddly, we don't hunger for this as Jesus did; he cherished alone time with his Father. It almost feels like we're afraid of what would happen if we got rid of every distraction. Consistent and extended (more than a few minutes) alone time with God and his Word is crucial to any maturing believer.

Stewardship

As each has received a gift, use it to serve one another, as good stewards of God's varied grace.

—1 Peter 4:10

Commit your work to the Lord, and your plans will be established.

—Proverbs 16:3

God has entrusted us with a lot of things. Whether it's money, our talents, or our time, we must use whatever God has given us wisely. Whatever we have should be used to advance the Kingdom of God instead of seeking momentary pleasures.

Scripture Memory

I have stored up your word in my heart, that I might not sin against you.

—Psalm 119:11

When we memorize Scripture, we have a ready defense against the temptations of this world. Studying the Word of God is extremely important, and so is not forgetting what it says. How else are we to be ready and willing to share the story of God? It's one thing to know where to find something in the Bible. It's an entirely different thing to have it written on your heart.

Fasting

And when you fast, do not look gloomy like the hypocrites, for they disfigure their faces that their fasting may be seen by others. Truly, I say to you, they have received their reward. But when you fast, anoint your head and wash your face, that your fasting may not be seen by others but by your Father who is in secret. And your Father who sees in secret will reward you.

—Matthew 6:16–18

Fasting has mostly been ignored by the majority of modern-day believers. In fasting, we are denying ourselves sustenance for a better and more lasting pursuit. In a day where the United States is the most well-fed nation in the world, it's hard to imagine what it would be like to completely rely on God for our physical provision. Through fasting, we are reminded that God is our provider who provides for us mentally, emotionally, physically, and spiritually. By fasting, we are giving up the material to focus on the spiritual.

Confession

Therefore, confess your sins to one another and pray for one another, that you may be healed. The prayer of a righteous person has great power as it is working.

—James 5:16

Confession brings freedom and an opportunity to live out the concept of forgiveness in our lives. We must learn to confess and be worthy of receiving someone else's confession. When we confess, it frees us from the guilt and power of sin in our lives. The path of repentance and restoration stems from our own confessions. When we graciously receive someone else's confession, we openly live out the reality of grace and mercy shown to us by God when he forgave us our sins.

Celebration

> And bring the fattened calf and kill it, and let us eat and
> celebrate.
>
> —Luke 15:23

Like the father who welcomed the prodigal home, we need
to celebrate the things God does in our lives and the lives of
others. We celebrate to remind ourselves God has already won
the war for our souls. We can never truly live in defeat because
the battle has already been won. Learning to celebrate means
living in God's victory over sin and death.

Journaling

> You shall therefore lay up these words of mine in your
> heart and in your soul, and you shall bind them as a sign
> on your hand, and they shall be as frontlets between your
> eyes. You shall teach them to your children, talking of
> them when you are sitting in your house, and when you
> are walking by the way, and when you lie down, and when
> you rise. You shall write them on the doorposts of your
> house and on your gates, that your days and the days of
> your children may be multiplied in the land that the Lord
> swore to your fathers to give them, as long as the heavens
> are above the earth.
>
> —Deuteronomy 11:18–21

There's something about writing down Scripture, prayers,
and thoughts that helps us contemplate the things of Jesus. This
goes far beyond a diary, which focuses on your own feelings.
Journaling reminds us of God's promises and his faithfulness
to see things through.

Meditation

> This Book of the Law shall not depart from your mouth, but you shall meditate on it day and night, so that you may be careful to do according to all that is written in it. For then you will make your way prosperous, and then you will have good success.
>
> —Joshua 1:8

One of the best illustrations I have ever heard about meditating on God's Word starts with a cow. The cow has four stomachs and undergoes a special digestive process to break down the tough and coarse food it eats. When the cow first eats, it chews the food just enough to swallow it. The unchewed food travels to the first two stomachs, where it is stored until later. When the cow is full, she rests. Later, the cow coughs up bits of the partly digested food called cud and chews it completely before swallowing it again. The cud then goes to the third and fourth stomachs, where it is fully digested. Some of this digested food enters the bloodstream and travels to a bag called the udder, where it is made into milk, while the rest goes towards the cow's nourishment.

What an awesome picture of meditation, which is good for service in the Kingdom of God and our own nourishment! Meditating is different from reading Scripture because the intent is to pour over a certain verse or passage for an extended time, "coughing" it up over and over again to get the full nourishment. In other words, it's OK to read things in Scripture more than once. Let it marinate in your mind over a few hours or even a few days!

The Discipler and the Concept of "Withness"

The idea of "withness" finds its greatest example in Jesus. He was always with his disciples. He poured his life into them, giving everything he was and making himself available at the most inconvenient of times. Sharing your life should never be separated from sharing the gospel. Paul spoke of this in his first letter to the church in Thessalonica:

> So, being affectionately desirous of you, we were ready to share with you not only the gospel of God but also our own selves, because you had become very dear to us.
>
> —1 Thessalonians 2:8

Paul knew that people needed an example to go and make disciples. They needed someone to teach them what it meant to chase after Jesus. I believe Scripture teaches us that every disciple is also a discipler and that they should pour into others. Making disciples means multiplying followers of Jesus in your area of influence, creating disciples who hear and obey God to give their maximum worship back to God. We make disciples and dedicate our lives to others, so they look more like Jesus.

This world drags everyone in a million different directions. People want influence over others, so they'll claim to speak the truth while secretly fulfilling their own selfish agendas. The idea of "withness" is crucial to disciple-making for this very reason. In order to catch the counterfeit, you have to show them the real thing.

> And what you have heard from me in the presence of many witnesses entrust to faithful men who will be able to teach others also.
>
> —2 Timothy 2:2

Disciple-making is more than a program; it requires your entire being. I fully admit how difficult this is within our current culture! We've convinced ourselves that we're either too busy or too inadequate to actually do what God has called us to do.

Disciples are not born into families. They are made through the power of the Holy Spirit, the hard work of an individual believer, and the diligence of mature believers who fulfill their roles as disciple-makers. It's how Jesus made disciples, and it's how the image of God is restored in people today.

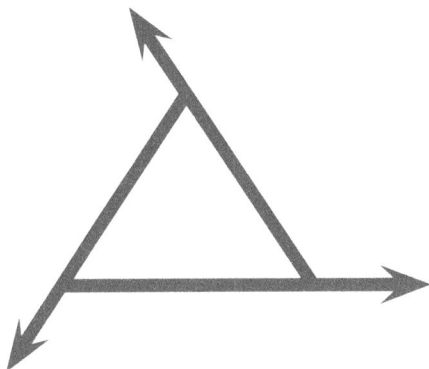

CHAPTER THREE

My Part in Restoring the Imago Dei

What Is a Disciple?

In Matthew 10, after a rousing reminder of the persecution every believer will endure, Jesus makes a general statement about disciples. In verses 24–25, he says, "A disciple is not above his teacher, nor a servant above his master. It is enough for the disciple to be like his teacher and the servant like his master." This general statement applies to the previous conversation about persecution in Matthew 10, but it also directly deals with a fundamental issue for being a disciple. We must imitate Jesus.

Jesus correlated being a disciple with pursuing the perfection of the Father and thereby pursuing him. For example, while teaching his disciples to love their enemies, in Matthew 5:48 he proclaims, "You therefore must be perfect, as your heavenly Father is perfect." Jesus obviously was making a statement that goes beyond the issue of loving our enemies.

The pursuit of perfection encompasses what it means to be a disciple.

Before we throw up our hands in defeat and lament our own imperfection, remember that Scripture never portrays true disciples as perfect people. Instead, disciples strive for the perfection found in Christ. They have the willingness to hear the things of God and put them into practice. Jesus plainly states in John 14:15, "If you love me, you will keep my commandments." Faithful disciples keep their eyes on Jesus.

In the Old Testament, God demands obedience from his people. Israel was judged on whether or not they were obeying God as a cohesive body. In his conversation with Nicodemus, Jesus explains in John 3:35–36, "The Father loves the Son and has given all things into his hand. Whoever believes in the Son has eternal life; whoever does not obey the Son shall not see life, but the wrath of God remains on him." A true disciple of Jesus embraces obedience. James describes obedience to God's Word as an active response.

> But be doers of the word, and not hearers only, deceiving yourselves. For if anyone is a hearer of the word and not a doer, he is like a man who looks intently at his natural face in the mirror. For he looks at himself and goes away and at once forgets what he was like. But the one who looks into the perfect law, the law of liberty, and perseveres, being no hearer who forgets but a doer who acts, he will be blessed in his doing.
>
> —James 1:22–25

A disciple hears and obeys. Anything less is unacceptable; a desire for anything other than complete surrender belittles the call of Jesus.

A Word of Caution

While the prospect of following the creator of everything into complete victory sounds incredible, most people find obedience to be in direct opposition to the life of luxury and ease they're currently pursuing. In reality, their concept of true happiness often differs from the outcome of true obedience. We're told that our obedience to Christ will bring persecution in some form or fashion. If we don't accept the possibility of persecution now, we'll fall into despair when things get tough later. Following Jesus is hard, and it requires more than most are willing to give.

> Now great crowds accompanied him, and he turned and said to them, "If anyone comes to me and does not hate his own father and mother and wife and children and brothers and sisters, yes, and even his own life, he cannot be my disciple. Whoever does not bear his own cross and come after me cannot be my disciple. For which of you, desiring to build a tower, does not first sit down and count the cost, whether he has enough to complete it? Otherwise, when he has laid a foundation and is not able to finish, all who see it begin to mock him, saying, 'This man began to build and was not able to finish.' Or what king, going out to encounter another king in war, will not sit down first and deliberate whether he is able with ten thousand to meet him who comes against him with twenty thousand? And if not, while the other is yet a great way off, he sends a delegation and asks for terms of peace. So therefore, any one of you who does not renounce all that he has cannot be my disciple.
>
> —Luke 14:25–33

In other words, count the cost before starting the journey. Right now, we can say it's all worth it because we may not be in a difficult time, but our circumstances can change in a heartbeat. During hard times, we need to remind ourselves that following Jesus is worth the effort. This is why disciple-making makes so much sense. We don't have to do this alone. We have the Holy Spirit and those who are discipling us to help along the way.

> For I consider that the sufferings of this present time are not worth comparing with the glory that is to be revealed to us. For the creation waits with eager longing for the revealing of the sons of God. For the creation was subjected to futility, not willingly, but because of him who subjected it, in hope that the creation itself will be set free from its bondage to corruption and obtain the freedom of the glory of the children of God. For we know that the whole creation has been groaning together in the pains of childbirth until now. And not only the creation, but we, who have the firstfruits of the Spirit, groan inwardly as we wait eagerly for adoption as sons, the redemption of our bodies. For in this hope we were saved. Now hope that is seen is not hope. For who hopes for what he sees? But if we hope for what we do not see, we wait for it with patience.

> Likewise the Spirit helps us in our weakness. For we do not know what to pray for as we ought, but the Spirit himself intercedes for us with groanings too deep for words. And he who searches hearts knows what is the mind of the Spirit, because the Spirit intercedes for the saints according to the will of God. And we know that for those who love God all things work together

for good, for those who are called according to his purpose.

—Romans 8:18–28

Our struggles only make sense when seen through God's point of view. He created us, saved us, knows us, and wants to use us for his glory. He wants to use us to advance his Kingdom here on earth, and it won't be easy considering we are surrounded by sinful people amid a broken world. Following Jesus will cost us everything, and that includes our own broken hopes and dreams.

Seeking the Kingdom

The Kingdom of God isn't some abstract concept Jesus talked about while he was here on earth. He initiated his Kingdom in a very real way, and it's a Kingdom unlike any other. Jesus turned the world upside down and showed people what it truly meant to live out the Imago Dei. In Matthew 6:33, Jesus says, "But seek first the kingdom of God and his righteousness, and all these things will be added to you." Obedience is essential in the Kingdom.

As believers, sometimes we pursue things considered to be good and moral, but we do so outside the framework of the Kingdom. Without allowing the Kingdom to define what is good and moral, our pursuit is tainted by the ebb and flow of culture. Local churches tend to be at odds with the Kingdom simply because they're a fraction of a degree off from their true goal. In other words, while the goal should be the Kingdom, it often becomes some other "good thing," ultimately causing believers to settle for less.

For example, I have seen many churches grow their congregations at the expense of missing the Kingdom. They get bigger churches, but the Kingdom of God never grows. People are drawn to a building, but disciples are not made. The local church can be an amazing and beautiful thing, but it's not the goal. If we pursue the local church, it's possible to miss the Kingdom altogether, but if we pursue the Kingdom, the local church flourishes in the pursuit of making disciples.

Most people who read Matthew 6:33 focus on what is promised ("all these things") more than the command to seek the Kingdom. By doing so, our understanding of what is best for God's Kingdom often collides violently with the truth of Scripture. The sole mission of this verse and of our lives as Christians is the Kingdom. Anything God gives us as a reward for our pursuit of the Kingdom is grace. The Kingdom is the goal, and Jesus is our prize. A true disciple seeks the Kingdom of God.

The Greatest Commandment and Commission

A group of Pharisees asked Jesus which was the greatest commandment, and he didn't hesitate to answer. In Matthew 22:37–40 Jesus explains:

> You shall love the Lord your God with all your heart and with all your soul and with all your mind. This is the great and first commandment. And a second is like it: You shall love your neighbor as yourself. These two commandments depend on all the Law and the Prophets.

If a disciple hears and obeys, this passage is a roadmap to success. Jesus claims all the commands of Scripture can be summed up in these two. Consequently, the rest of Scripture fleshes out these commandments.

Loving God

In our modern-day understanding of following Jesus, we often divide things into manageable pieces. We feel like compartmentalizing our lives and having everything measured out promises a smooth life. Unfortunately, Jesus's lordship over our lives can't be controlled, and we can't fragment our love for God by only allowing him to influence the parts of our lives we deem acceptable. Love is about completion, not compartmentalization.

> You shall love the Lord your God with all your heart and with all your soul and with all your mind.
>
> —Matthew 22:37

First-century Jews would not have understood Jesus's command to love God as doing so with three distinct parts of their being. If our love is compartmentalized, some might argue they love God with their hearts, but not with their minds. Such a statement sounds crazy. The heart, soul, and mind are not three different parts of man. If anything, Jesus's explanation shows how completely we should love God.

Don't miss the foundational truth of this verse. Loving God means we obey his commandments. Seeking his Kingdom translates to obedience because the Kingdom is the ultimate goal. In other words, we love God the best by being a disciple. A disciple hears and obeys. If we love God, we're going to hear and obey his commandments. That is what it means to love him with all our hearts, soul, and mind. We obey him. Anything else risks overcomplicating the issue. I love God completely by being his disciple and obeying his commandments.

Loving People

The Bible is very clear on what it means to love people. Take for example two specific instances in Scripture. The first we find in the book of Luke.

> On one of those days, as he was teaching, Pharisees and teachers of the law were sitting there, who had come from every village of Galilee and Judea and from Jerusalem. And the power of the Lord was with him to heal. And behold, some men were bringing on a bed a man who was paralyzed, and they were seeking to bring him in and lay him before Jesus, but finding no way to bring him in, because of the crowd, they went up on the roof and let him down with his bed through the tiles into the midst before Jesus. And when he saw their faith, he said, "Man, your sins are forgiven you." And the scribes and the Pharisees began to question, saying, "Who is this who speaks blasphemies? Who can forgive sins but God alone?" When Jesus perceived their thoughts, he answered them, "Why do you question in your hearts? Which is easier, to say, 'Your sins are forgiven you,' or to say, 'Rise and walk'? But that you may know that the Son of Man has authority on earth to forgive sins"—he said to the man who was paralyzed— "I say to you, rise, pick up your bed and go home." And immediately he rose up before them and picked up what he had been lying on and went home, glorifying God. And amazement seized them all, and they glorified God and were filled with awe, saying, "We have seen extraordinary things today."
>
> —Luke 5:17–26

The best way for Jesus to love a paralyzed man was to forgive his sins. Jesus healed many people in response to their faith, but here he purposely draws a distinction between physical and spiritual healing. The man's sin problem outweighed his physical problem. Jesus's love for man would not be any less if he had chosen to forgive his sins and walk away. So often we deal with the tangible problems in front of our eyes "in the name of Jesus" instead of putting all our energy into the more devastating wound of sin. If you want to love people, give them Jesus, not just help in the name of Jesus.

The physical needs of others are vastly important, but they are not eternally important. We must provide for the physical needs of others, but never at the expense of their spiritual need. Loving others means sharing the gospel and making disciples. Take a look at another story in Acts. Here, we find an example of meeting physical needs while sharing the gospel.

> Now Peter and John were going up to the temple at the hour of prayer, the ninth hour. And a man lame from birth was being carried, whom they laid daily at the gate of the temple that is called the Beautiful Gate to ask alms of those entering the temple. Seeing Peter and John about to go into the temple, he asked to receive alms. And Peter directed his gaze at him, as did John, and said, "Look at us." And he fixed his attention on them, expecting to receive something from them. But Peter said, "I have no silver and gold, but what I do have I give to you. In the name of Jesus Christ of Nazareth, rise up and walk!" And he took him by the right hand and raised him up, and immediately his feet and ankles were made strong. And leaping up he stood and began to walk, and entered the temple with them, walking and leaping and praising God. And all the people saw him walking and praising God and recognized him as the one who sat at the Beautiful Gate of the temple, asking for alms. And they were

filled with wonder and amazement at what had happened to him.

While he clung to Peter and John, all the people, utterly astounded, ran together to them in the portico called Solomon's. And when Peter saw it he addressed the people: "Men of Israel, why do you wonder at this, or why do you stare at us, as though by our own power or piety we have made him walk?

—Acts 3:1–12

A man was healed, and the gospel was proclaimed. Peter and John loved people! We should never try to love others solely by giving them things a local charity could provide. We have the gospel. The most loving thing we can do is go and make disciples of Jesus Christ.

PART TWO

WHY DISCIPLE-MAKING MAKES SENSE

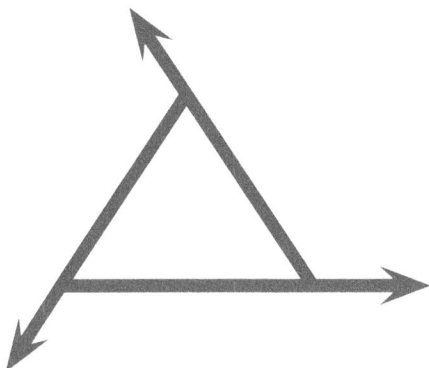

CHAPTER FOUR

Why Should I Make Disciples?

Creation and the Great Commission

When we talk about the Great Commission, we often plant our feet in the New Testament and stay there. However, another powerful revelation comes in Genesis, where God commands his children to make disciples from the very beginning. The first two chapters of Genesis paint a beautiful picture of his purpose for humanity.

> Then God said, "Let us make man in our image, after our likeness. And let them have dominion over the fish of the sea and over the birds of the heavens and over the livestock and over all the earth and over every creeping thing that creeps on the earth." So God created man in his own image, in the image of God he created him; male and female he created them. And God blessed them. And God said to them, "Be fruitful and multiply and fill the

earth and subdue it, and have dominion over the fish of
the sea and over the birds of the heavens and over every
living thing that moves on the earth."

—Genesis 1:26–28

When God created Adam and Eve, he made them special,
set apart from everything else he had spoken into existence.
They were made in God's image. Nothing else he created was
given such an intimate conception.

Then the Lord God formed the man of dust from the
ground and breathed into his nostrils the breath of life,
and the man became a living creature.

—Genesis 2:7

Nowhere else in the creation account can you find such a
personal touch from God. Everything else was spoken into
existence, but Adam was formed and fashioned by God's own
hands. Even more miraculous, God physically breathed the
breath of life into him. Whatever purpose God had for creation,
humanity was his chosen instrument to fulfill it. For example,
look at how and why God created Eve.

Then the Lord God said, "It is not good that the man
should be alone; I will make him a helper fit for him."
Now out of the ground the Lord God had formed every
beast of the field and every bird of the heavens and
brought them to man to see what he would call them.
And whatever the man called every living creature, that
was its name. The man gave names to all the livestock and
to the birds of the heavens and to every beast of the field.
But for Adam, there was not found a helper fit for him.
So the Lord God caused a deep sleep to fall upon the man,

and while he slept took one of his ribs and closed up its place with flesh. And the rib that the Lord God had taken from the man he made into a woman and brought her to the man.

—Genesis 2:18–22

Most readers would say Adam needed companionship, but if you look closely at the Scripture, God didn't create Eve because Adam was lonely. It says that Adam was alone, not lonely. Truthfully, Adam experienced a perfect relationship with his Creator and desired for nothing else. Eve was not made to complete Adam as a person, but God, in his sovereignty, knew Adam needed Eve to accomplish what he planned for humanity.

The Lord God took the man and put him in the garden of Eden to work it and keep it.

—Genesis 2:15

If we're not careful here, the original meaning of the passage can be lost in translation. The Hebrew is actually quite beautiful and unique. "Work it and keep it" is an odd phrase when taken by itself, especially since we don't find another like it anywhere else in Scripture. Old Testament scholar John Sailhamer points out a vastly important nuance in this phrase. A more suitable translation for the Hebrew words, *abad* and *shamar*, would be "to worship and obey." In other words, God created Adam and Eve to reflect his image and placed them in the garden to worship their creator through obedience![4] Now, we need to go

---

4   John H. Sailhamer, "Genesis" in *The Expositor's Bible Commentary*, ed. Frank E. Gaebelein (Grand Rapids, MI: Zondervan, 1990), 45.

back to Genesis 1:28. Remember, sin has not entered the world yet.

> And God blessed them. And God said to them, "Be fruitful and multiply and fill the earth and subdue it, and have dominion over the fish of the sea and over the birds of the heavens and over every living thing that moves on the earth."
>
> —Genesis 1:28

In other words, God created Adam and Eve and put them in the garden to worship him forever through obedience. He commanded them to be fruitful and multiply. God desired to see the entire world filled with people made in his image who would worship him forever, and he gave Adam and Eve the responsibility of multiplying disciples long before Jesus ever uttered the Great Commission.

If Adam and Eve had chosen to worship and obey God perfectly, the need to make disciples would have still existed. God's plan for humanity did not change when sin entered the world. Clearly, the need to make disciples through procreation would have remained, even in a perfect existence.

God's plan for humanity could not be undone by any sinful actions. Adam and Eve were created to worship God through obedience by multiplying disciples who would worship and obey him. In one of the most amazing signs of grace, our purpose has remained despite our sins.

We don't need to look for the Great Commission solely in the New Testament. God's purpose for his creation, and especially humanity, can be seen in Genesis 1. Making disciples wasn't God's backup plan. He wove the reality of disciple-making into the fabric of our existence, and, through grace, allows us to continue with our original purpose intact.

Sin taints our worship of God. It twists and distorts our perfect existence; however, through Jesus's death and resurrection, we are forgiven of our sins in the past, present, and future. The Holy Spirit changes us daily, reordering our worship away from the things of this world and back to God. This is what it means to make disciples.

The Great Commission

The last thing Jesus verbalized to his disciples was his command for them to go and make more disciples. We always give attention to the last words, and rightly so. We would expect the final words of Jesus to be of the utmost importance, and he fulfilled that expectation with Matthew 28:18–20. Jesus meant for the Great Commission to pertain to all believers, including those who would come long after his ascension. Jesus often thought of all the people who would follow him in the future, including all of us who are pursuing him right now.

> But now I am coming to you, and these things I speak in the world, that they may have my joy fulfilled in themselves. I have given them your word, and the world has hated them because they are not of the world, just as I am not of the world. I do not ask that you take them out of the world, but that you keep them from the evil one. They are not of the world, just as I am not of the world. Sanctify them in the truth; your word is truth. As you sent me into the world, so I have sent them into the world. And for their sake, I consecrate myself, that they also may be sanctified in truth. I do not ask for these only, but also for those who will believe in me through their word, that they may all be one, just as you, Father, are in

me, and I in you, that they also may be in us, so that the world may believe that you have sent me.

—John 17:13–21

Everyone who follows Jesus bears the responsibility of proclaiming truth and multiplying disciples. Unfortunately, our churches have convinced believers that most of the Kingdom's work should be done by highly educated and experienced pastors instead of the much less competent people sitting in the chairs (or pews if you still have those). In actuality, it is the responsibility of pastors to equip *all* believers to make disciples. This is the work of the church.

And he gave the apostles, the prophets, the evangelists, the shepherds, and teachers, to equip the saints for the work of ministry, for building up the body of Christ, until we all attain to the unity of the faith and of the knowledge of the Son of God, to mature manhood, to the measure of the stature of the fullness of Christ, so that we may no longer be children, tossed to and fro by the waves and carried about by every wind of doctrine, by human cunning, by craftiness in deceitful schemes. Rather, speaking the truth in love, we are to grow up in every way into him who is the head, into Christ, from whom the whole body, joined and held together by every joint with which it is equipped, when each part is working properly, makes the body grow so that it builds itself up in love.

—Ephesians 4:11–16

Making disciples is the responsibility of the church, not the pastors. If pastors don't specifically equip members to multiply followers of Jesus, they aren't doing what God has called them to do. All believers have been commissioned to make disciples.

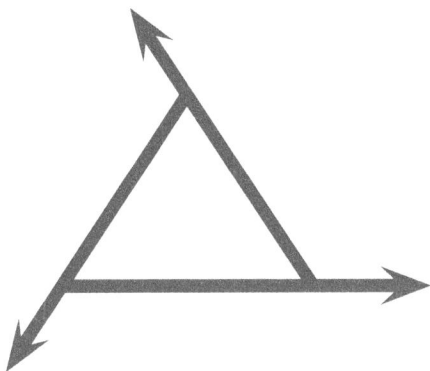

CHAPTER FIVE

The One True Catalyst

Having children is one of the greatest blessings, dating all the way back to God's command for Adam and Eve to be fruitful and multiply. Although it is never easy, the joy of loving and raising one of God's creations is ultimately indescribable. I have two children, Ellie and Brecken. Ellie has been exceeding parental expectations ever since she was born. She could sing before she could talk; she loves to read and genuinely cares for people on a deep and intimate level. Brecken is, by far, the sweetest little boy you could ever imagine. I'm not sure how he does it, but he instinctively knows when to crawl up in my lap and just sit there. Even at an early age, he chose to lay down his life for others and put their interests above his own.

Brecken and Ellie are amazing children, but even the most amazing children are still broken by sin. This means that Ellie sometimes lies to get what she wants, and Brecken actively searches for ways to do the least amount of work possible. They scream at each other and get into verbal sparring matches. At times, those verbal attacks turn physical, resulting in a thrown punch or jiujitsu-style takedown. In such situations, my wife, Angie, and I step in and lay down the law. The law usually takes the form of household rules. As a young parent, you realize early on that such rules are a necessity. "Don't punch your brother or sister" quickly becomes a standard rule to keep the peace.

I remember one time I walked into a room and saw Ellie with her back to Brecken. To this day I'm not sure what had transpired before my arrival, but unbeknownst to Ellie, Brecken was in full "swing mode." He had his arm cocked back ready to punch his sister with all his might. As his fist came down, I screamed at the top of my lungs, "We don't hit our sister!" Brecken stopped and looked up at me. Ellie, finally realizing I had saved her from a copious amount of pain, began to cry. Brecken, seeing his sister burst into tears followed suit and promptly began to shed a massive number of tears as well. It was a chaotic scenario, one that has probably played out for centuries in households all over the world.

As I sat there and comforted both my children, I looked Brecken in the face. At that moment I saw something that changed the way I would parent. Brecken still wanted to hit his sister. You could see it in his eyes. The pain from whatever had occurred still remained, and he wanted to unleash it on someone else. My interference may have stopped him for the time being, but it didn't change his desire.

In a world created by God, filled with godless people, it finally all made sense to me. You can't legislate morality. Rules may curb certain barbaric tendencies, but they'll never change the heart. Rules alone will never be a catalyst for true change. Real change requires a change of heart, and a change of heart requires disciple-making. From a biblical perspective, making disciples is the one true catalyst for change in this world that has an eternal impact. In other words, we've been going about this the wrong way.

Rules Don't Change the Heart

Rules, by themselves, will never change the way someone thinks. We must allow God to change the way we think before rules make sense to us. In his letter to the church in Rome, Paul talks about change occurring when we allow God to take over.

> I appeal to you, therefore, brothers, by the mercies of God, to present your bodies as a living sacrifice, holy and acceptable to God, which is your spiritual worship. Do not be conformed to this world, but be transformed by the renewal of your mind, that by testing you may discern what is the will of God, what is good and acceptable and perfect.
>
> —Romans 12:1–2

Only God can renew our minds. Before we're able to discern the will of God, we have to change the way we think. When we allow God to change the way we think, we change completely because he changes our hearts. If we're not careful, we can change what we do without changing who we are. We'll only look more like Jesus when we think more like Jesus.

When I tell my son, "We don't hit our sister," he immediately stops, but it takes time to change the way he thinks. I'm not in the business of raising my children to be rule-followers. I don't want Brecken to stop hitting Ellie just because I caught him in the act. I want him to love his sister completely, and that takes a heart transformation I can't accomplish on my own. If my son isn't radically transformed by the power of the Holy Spirit, in partnership with my dedication to disciple him, his life will be defined by brokenness.

The Futility of Activism

I've lived long enough to realize that everything won't go the way I want it to go. I've battled through depression, anxiety, fear, and ambivalence and finally come to the conclusion that this world is even more messed up than I originally thought. When we see something that doesn't make sense, our instinct is to cry out for justice. Everyone who's been wronged knows the pain of betrayal and the desire for restitution. We may not understand the pain of an individual in a specific situation, but the feeling of helplessness is universal. Sometimes, bad things happen to us because of the actions of other people.

As broken people, we've all victimized others at one time or another, but let's concentrate on our own pain for the time being. All movements in this world, great and horrible alike, have been birthed out of a desire for change. Sometimes, we seek to fight injustice, but other times we simply want our lives to improve. In most instances over the past century, social activists have risen up and fought for the oppressed. Activism is simply the action or deeds of people to bring about change. No matter how big or small the cause, activism is the go-to method for instigating a culture shift.

Activism might bring about change, but it doesn't guarantee a change of heart. Even if a change of heart occurs, that doesn't guarantee a change in the eternal destination for an individual. Only God, through his grace and power, can save us from ourselves. Our responsibility as Christians isn't to bring about social change. We've been called to make disciples. It's possible to bring about social change but never make a disciple of Jesus;

however, if we make a disciple, social change should quickly follow.

The Delusion of Doing "Good"

In talking with most church leaders, I find a concerning trend in what they expect from people in their congregations. I was having a conversation with a senior pastor about the role of the church in the world today, and I asked him how he measured success among his people. The next thirty minutes were filled with descriptions of a variety of service projects: taking food to people in need, surprising first responders with gift cards, congregants running for office and pushing through conservative legislation, and numerous other accomplishments (most of them quite impressive). He even bragged that he didn't have to teach his people to do any of these things. My friend claimed it was a natural outpouring of what it means to be a follower of Christ. In other words, the people in his church were responsible, and often compassionate, citizens. For him, the church's good reputation in the community was proof enough they were doing what God had called them to do. They were doing "good."

As I drove home, I pondered the idea of "doing good" and tried to wrap my head around the biblical equivalent. Obviously, Scripture speaks about us being good citizens, and there was nothing wrong with what my friend's church was doing; however, I couldn't shake the feeling that something was off about his assessment of what is truly good.

Jesus's ultimate command for his church is found in the Great Commission. Making disciples is the ministry of the church, and we can't replace that with anything else. If we were created in Christ Jesus for good works, those "good works" must coincide with our true purpose.

For by grace you have been saved through faith. And
this is not your own doing; it is the gift of God, not a
result of works, so that no one may boast. For we are his
workmanship, created in Christ Jesus for good works,
which God prepared beforehand, that we should walk in
them.

—Ephesians 2:8–10

At the very least, our salvation and our good works are
inseparable because one makes the other possible. If salvation
allows us to grow in Christ, then we are finally capable, through
the leading of the Spirit, to fulfill what we were created to do
since the beginning of time: make disciples. God planned the
crucifixion of Jesus and the redemption of those who would
believe. Peter stated as much at Pentecost:

Men of Israel, hear these words: Jesus of Nazareth, a man
attested to you by God with mighty works and wonders
and signs that God did through him in your midst, as you
yourselves know—this Jesus, delivered up according to
the definite plan and foreknowledge of God, you crucified
and killed by the hands of lawless men. God raised him
up, loosing the pangs of death, because it was not possible
for him to be held by it.

—Acts 2:22–24

God purposefully designed us with the death of his Son in
mind. Redemption and, by default, the church's role in the
reconciliation of creation was planned from the very beginning
of all things. Paul, in a lengthier passage, expresses the same
reality in his letter to the Ephesians. God knew he wanted
Jesus to die on the cross. He wanted to save us and desired his
children to play a part in the reconciliation of all things.

Blessed be the God and Father of our Lord Jesus Christ, who has blessed us in Christ with every spiritual blessing in the heavenly places, even as he chose us in him before the foundation of the world, that we should be holy and blameless before him. In love, he predestined us for adoption to himself as sons through Jesus Christ, according to the purpose of his will, to the praise of his glorious grace, with which he has blessed us in the Beloved. In him we have redemption through his blood, the forgiveness of our trespasses according to the riches of this grace, which he lavished upon us, in all wisdom and insight making known to us the mystery of his will, according to his purpose, which he outlined in Christ as a plan for the fullness of time, to unite all things in him, things in heaven and things on earth. In him we have obtained an inheritance, having been predestined according to the purpose of him who works all things according to the counsel of his will, so that we who were the first to hope in Christ might be to the praise of his glory.

In him you also, when you heard the word of truth, the gospel of your salvation, and believed in him, were sealed with the promised Holy Spirit, who is the guarantee of our inheritance until we acquire possession of it, to the praise of his glory.

—Ephesians 1:3–14

If God determined that Jesus would die, it makes sense he also planned what we would do as his children to advance the gospel. Taking Scripture as a whole, it seems pretty apparent that whatever "good works" we do, they are wrapped up in the Great Commission and Jesus's command for our lives. Good works are used by the Holy Spirit in our efforts to go and make disciples.

Jesus knew our lives on earth would point to something. As Christians, we should unapologetically point people to Christ as we do the work of reconciliation. If we're not careful, we might end up doing good things in the eyes of the world and never make an impact for the Kingdom of God. As believers, our good works have the end goal of making disciples

> "You are the salt of the earth, but if salt has lost its taste, how shall its saltiness be restored? It is no longer good for anything except to be thrown out and trampled under people's feet. You are the light of the world. A city set on a hill cannot be hidden. Nor do people light a lamp and put it under a basket, but on a stand, and it gives light to all in the house. In the same way, let your light shine before others, so that they may see your good works and give glory to your Father who is in heaven."
>
> —Matthew 5:13–16

Doing good has to mean more than our shallow understanding of the concept. Scripture teaches that good works must have an eternal component to them, which means making disciples is intrinsically good. However, things we consider to be good with no eternal impact aren't really good at all. Unfortunately, I can do good works without making disciples, but I can't make disciples without doing good because making disciples is inherently good. Therefore, we should focus all our energy on making disciples.

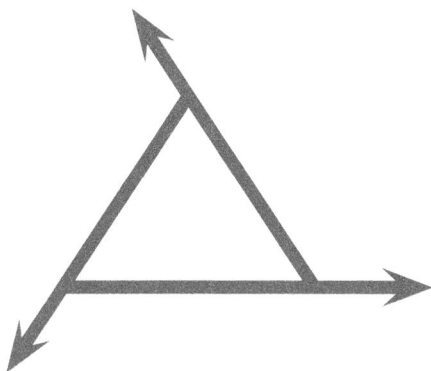

CHAPTER SIX

The Absurdity of Grace

We live in a world where grace doesn't blend well with our current culture. In fact, most people lack the personal experience to realistically fathom the true meaning of grace. In other words, when grace is scarce or deemphasized, people will understand it less. While some think God's grace doesn't fit in a world where people would rather forsake him and seek their own pleasure, I believe Scripture teaches the opposite. The crazier this world gets, the more God's grace makes sense. In fact, I would argue that grace is the only way God gets what he wants.

God wants to fill this world with people who worship him. Remember, Adam and Eve were placed in the garden to *abad* and *shamar*, or worship and obey. However, because of our own propensity for sin and destruction, it's impossible to choose God on our own. God had to make an active choice to help us fulfill our purpose in life.

What God Desires Above All

I remember walking around the University of Costa Rica with my guide, Nico, who was kind and accommodating, which meant he was patient enough to answer all my inane questions. After walking around for most of the day, we came upon a large spherical object surrounded by a temporary, albeit sturdy, plexiglass structure. It looked like a modern work of art, but Nico explained that it was an ancient artifact from a people group known as the Diquis. I was immediately intrigued; I love learning about ancient cultures and structures. When I asked Nico what it represented, he informed me that no one really knows. In fact, since their discovery, the Diquis Spheres and their purpose have been shrouded in mystery.

Like any other historical conundrum, theories abound. Most historians believe the spheres were used for ancient astrological purposes, but there are more outlandish theories that include aliens, kings, and human sacrifices. In such a scenario, you have to wonder how easy it would have been for the creators of the spheres to simply write down their purpose. A simple note would have sufficed, but alas, none has survived. Once again, purpose eludes us.

Purpose is an interesting concept, especially when it comes to the motivations of God. Why did God create everything? The foolishness of believing God needed to legitimize his own existence to anyone often clouds our understanding; however, if God didn't need to prove anything to anyone, why the effort to create intelligent life? There must be a foundational truth to why God created everything that exists, and we must look to Scripture to find our answer.

Above all, God desires his own glory, and humanity is intrinsically connected to his greatness. The prophet Isaiah lays out a very emphatic explanation for the creation of God's people and why he keeps them around even after they continue to rebel. Look at what the prophet Isaiah writes:

> For my name's sake I defer my anger; for the sake of my praise I restrain it for you, that I may not cut you off. Behold, I have refined you, but not as silver; I have tried you in the furnace of affliction. For my own sake, for my own sake, I do it, for how should my name be profaned? My glory I will not give to another.
>
> —Isaiah 48:9–11

When I'm speaking with people who are "seeking" or "trying out" Christianity, they have many questions about the nature of God, and one of the main sticking points for some tends to be God's pursuit of his own glory. They misunderstand God's purpose for humanity and falsely assume that God is a mean-spirited being who creates intelligent beings and forces them to live in servitude. However, nothing is further from the truth. In fact, the previous line of thought comes across as illogical when considering our propensity for egocentrism. In other words, if God created the world for his own glory, the only way we will experience the greatest joy is by living for God's majesty and splendor. God made us to worship him forever, which is why our greatest happiness will always be wrapped up in who he is and what he has planned for us.

In Isaiah 48:11, God repeats, "for my own sake," and the metanarrative of Scripture resounds with this truth: God created everything for his own pleasure, as expressed in Colossians 1:16 where Paul proclaims, "all things were created through him and for him." Everything created exists by God's hand and for his glory.

God's Desire for Humanity

If God's greatest desire is for his own glory, humanity (God's greatest creation) must have a role to play in his plan. The prophet Isaiah makes it clear in 48:10 that God has a purpose for humanity. He explains, "Behold, I have refined you, but not as silver; I have tried you in the furnace of affliction." When we look at this truth from a metanarrative standpoint, we see the bigger picture and God's desire for his special creation. God created Adam and Eve in the garden to be fruitful and to multiply disciples, but God didn't throw away his purpose for humanity when sin entered the world. He is continually refining us amid our sin and rebellion for the purpose of his own glory.

Obviously, the best way for us to bring God the most glory is to live out our original purpose. Yes, we were created to be with God and enjoy him forever. This is an old refrain, and those called by God into his family will experience eternal bliss; however, in Scripture, God clearly lays out his earthly purpose for humanity. Jesus specifically trained the apostles to go and make disciples, and he expects us to do the same. We bring God the most glory when we obey him. Jesus said as much when speaking with his disciples:

> If you love me, you will keep my commandments. And I will ask the Father, and he will give you another Helper, to be with you forever, even the Spirit of truth, whom the world cannot receive, because it neither sees him nor knows him. You know him, for he dwells with you and will be in you. I will not leave you as orphans; I will come to you. Yet a little while and the world will see me no more, but you will see me. Because I live, you also will live. In that day you will know that I am in my Father, and you in me, and I in you. Whoever has my commandments

and keeps them, he it is who loves me. And he who loves me will be loved by my Father, and I will love him and manifest myself to him.

—John 14:15–21

We live our best lives when obeying and following the commands of Jesus. If Jesus charges us to go and make disciples, then we must do it with great joy and enthusiasm. Loving the Lord with all our heart, soul, mind, and strength means working hard to multiply followers of Jesus.

While we don't earn the love of God by obeying him, we unmistakably express our greatest love when we carry out his mission. Obedience is worship, and there is no worship without obedience. Simply acknowledging the attributes of God does not constitute true worship. Local churches are made up of people who sing praises to God every Sunday, but never truly worship him. Their words come up empty and void of any true significance solely based on their inability to follow through with conviction. God desires humanity for the purpose of advancing his Kingdom through making disciples, and in doing so, we bring him the most glory.

The Culture Choice

I love my wife with everything I am. I wish I could tell you that I've always been the best husband or made the right choices when it comes to showing her how much she means to me, but sadly, the opposite has been true too many times. One season of life, in particular, was very hard, and I walked a dark path that should have destroyed my spouse and children. When my struggles were revealed and light came bursting into my darkness, not many people stuck around. My wife showed me

Jesus when no one else did, and for that reason alone, she will always be a reminder of his grace to me.

When I needed help the most, the local church (including those I considered to be friends) never showed up. I promise this isn't an attempt to play the victim card; I know exactly what I did and how horrible it was. In this scenario, I wasn't the victim. I was the perpetrator, wrongdoer, offender, and villain. Everyone had every right to abandon me, but as the Church universal, they shouldn't have left us. What defines a believer is the refusal to let the darkness of sin twist how we see those around us, but that is not the culture of the world. The world would rather expunge from existence those it views as broken. Unfortunately, believers in our churches are buying into this practice and ignoring the character of Jesus in the process.

Disciple-making cannot exist without grace. If we continue to see the people around us as hindrances to our chosen lifestyle instead of valued creations of God, we will never accomplish what we were created for in perfection. Jesus loved everyone and had compassion for those lost in their own brokenness. Jesus told a beautiful parable illustrating this very concept.

> He also told this parable to some who trusted in themselves that they were righteous, and treated others with contempt: "Two men went up into the temple to pray, one a pharisee and the other a tax collector. The Pharisee, standing by himself, prayed thus: 'God, I thank you that I am not like other men, extortioners, unjust, adulterers, or even like this tax collector. I fast twice a week; I give tithes of all that I get.' But the tax collector, standing far off, would not even lift up his eyes to heaven, but beat his breast, saying, 'God, be merciful

to me, a sinner!' I tell you, this man went down to his house justified, rather than the other. For everyone who exalts himself will be humbled, but the one who humbles himself will be exalted."

—Luke 18:9–14

Most people do not practice grace. They do everything in their power to build themselves up and look down on those around them. We tend to judge people for different reasons. Sometimes, we simply think we're better than other people, having progressed more in our understanding and knowledge of how the world should run. Others we see as beneath our status, constantly blaming them for their deplorable station in life. As Christians, we often view people as irredeemable if they don't share our convictions, avoiding them at all costs or trying to legislate authority over their lives.

In today's culture, you only get one shot (or one mistake). Depending on how big your success or how miserable your failure is, we tend to cement a person's status as immovable and unchangeable. If someone wrongs us or those around us, we believe their punishment should be long-lasting and impossible to overcome. Only then will we truly find justice, and in our version of justice, there is no grace.

We are a one-and-done society that allows for no growth or redemption. When someone messes up, we're more concerned with punishment than we are with forgiveness or restoration, but without grace, we lose the very essence of God. If grace doesn't exist, we squander the opportunity for redemption, eliminating any chance to grow beyond our failures. Culture defies grace, so our lives as Christians should be different than the world around us. In other words, if your beliefs and values match up nicely with the rest of the world, chances are you have a skewed view of grace.

Herein lies the problem: if we espouse following the world's justice instead of the grace of God, we will never make disciples. Making disciples is all about growth, and there is no growth without grace. Making disciples must allow broken people to get better.

The apostle Peter's life is the perfect case study for grace and growth in disciple-making. Can you imagine what would have happened to Peter if Jesus had left him in his sin and shame after his denial? Instead, we get one of the most amazing stories of grace.

> When they had finished breakfast, Jesus said to Simon Peter, "Simon, son of John, do you love me more than these?" He said to him, "Yes, Lord; you know that I love you." He said to him, "Feed my lambs." He said to him a second time, "Simon, son of John, do you love me?" He said to him, "Yes, Lord; you know that I love you." He said to him, "Tend my sheep." He said to him the third time, "Simon, son of John, do you love me?" Peter was grieved because he said to him the third time, "Do you love me?" and he said to him, "Lord, you know everything; you know that I love you." Jesus said to him, "Feed my sheep."
>
> —John 21:25–17

Jesus had every right to think less of Peter. Justice would have dictated that Peter be punished in some form or fashion, but grace and purpose won the day. Peter's life would never be the same, and we see a difference in him from this point forward. There may be times when grace doesn't change people, but showing grace always models the character of Jesus.

Please don't take my words out of context. I am not arguing for a world without consequences. In fact, Scripture points to discipline as a great way of teaching and growing us as individuals. I understand the need for consequences, but our need to see the wicked punished should never outweigh our desire for true heart change in an individual. If the goal is always giving someone what they deserve, disciple-making is impossible.

Cultured Citizen vs. Immovable Ambassador

I hate politics. Anyone who knows me knows I have a massive distrust of any political process. When broken people put forth broken legislation, broken things happen. Being apolitical means people are never satisfied with my answer when they ask about my political affiliations. When I tell them I'm not a conservative, liberal, libertarian, anarchist, or progressive, they almost seem confused. At heart, I'm a Christian, which means I only have one driving force in my life: what has God revealed to me through Scripture, and how should I live my life accordingly? I don't fit into any other category because no label fully embraces what it means to follow Christ.

Cultures change all the time, which means laws and belief systems change with them. There will always be people who are dissatisfied with their current culture, especially if their personal beliefs don't match up with the majority. Politically speaking, this is where we get the term *progressive*. Progressives view themselves as agents for change; the problem is that there's no true standard for what is right and wrong with progressive ideology. Everything ebbs and flows with the changing culture. In this case, the majority (or sometimes the vocal minority) sets the stage for change. In other words, if we can get enough people to agree with us, we can change the culture and turn the world against those who refuse to change.

For true growth to take place, an established moral standard must exist. Without an absolute moral law, no one can ever know what is right or wrong. Without right and wrong, anyone can manipulate those around them to adopt their broken agenda, labeling those who don't as bigots and hypocrites.

This is why Christians have such a hard time in a changing culture. It has nothing to do with whether or not our country was founded on Christian principles (there are plenty of other ideologies mixed into our founding documents), but it has everything to do with the fact that our culture is always changing. Think about it this way: the Constitution of the United States of America allows the people to "amend" or change it. Scripture, however, never allows for such a thing. According to what God has revealed, there will always be a right and wrong answer to questions of morality.

Christianity stands in opposition to a continually changing culture for many reasons. First, God is unchanging. He is the living standard for perfection, and no one else in all of the creation gets to decide what is right or wrong. Second, the whole point of disciple-making is to progress toward the perfect standard set forth by Jesus Christ. If the standard kept changing, that would conflict with the idea of an unchanging God. Finally, growth requires grace. Without grace, there is no growth.

In a fluid culture, reconciliation isn't possible if the finish line keeps changing. This is a problem considering that God has given us the ministry of reconciliation.

> Therefore, if anyone is in Christ, he is a new creation. The old has passed away; behold, the new has come. All this is from God, who through Christ reconciled us to himself and gave us the ministry of reconciliation; that is,

in Christ God was reconciling the world to himself, not counting their trespasses against them, and entrusting to us the message of reconciliation. Therefore, we are ambassadors for Christ, God making his appeal through us. We implore you on behalf of Christ, be reconciled to God.

—2 Corinthians 5:17–20

We have been made in the image of God, so Jesus is the blueprint for our existence. His entire ministry was built on the idea of reconciliation. As the chosen vehicles for advancing his Kingdom, we must speak and live the reality of grace to everyone around us. Our purpose is to be immovable ambassadors in the middle of a progressive culture.

How God Gets What He Wants

In the end, the idea of God's grace seems absurd. He created us in perfection with the opportunity to be with him forever, and we chose to follow our own passions and forsake him. Even so, God chose to pursue his creation.

For while we were still weak, at the right time Christ died for the ungodly. For one will scarcely die for a righteous person—though perhaps for a good person one would dare even to die—but God shows his love for us in that while we were still sinners, Christ died for us.

—Romans 5:6–8

If it wasn't absurd, it wouldn't be grace. Grace is unmerited, unearned, and inexplicable within the realm of human understanding. It makes no sense for God to call us friends, and yet he does.

To truly understand what God wants, we must look to his perfect, created order. In Colossians 1:16, Paul reminds us, "For by him all things were created, in heaven and on earth, visible and invisible, whether thrones or dominions or rulers or authorities—all things were created through him and for him." Everything was created *for* him and for his glory.

For God to receive the most glory, he created a world where we choose whether or not to love him. In giving us this choice, he makes it possible for us to reject him and pursue our own wicked desires. Once we choose the wrong path, however, there is no turning back unless God intervenes. Thankfully, God chose to send his son, Jesus, to die for an unworthy creation, and herein lies the greatest of all miracles: If God created all things to bring him the most glory, grace is the only way he gets what he wants. Without his grace, it would be impossible for us to do anything of value.

PART THREE
THE BIBLICAL MODEL

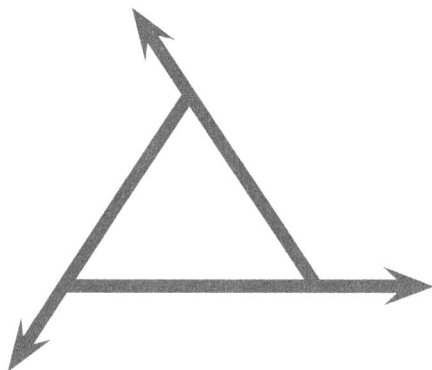

CHAPTER SEVEN
Remain

Jesus lingered with his disciples. He sought them out, gave them a purpose, and stayed with them as long as he walked this earth. His entire ministry centered on preparing twelve men to take over when he was gone. Jesus had a mission, one he accomplished in three years with the most unlikely of companions. The time he spent teaching, modeling, and coaching his disciples to advance the Kingdom of God made an eternal impact. Discipling them was more important than anything else. We know this because that's exactly what he did almost all the time during the last three years of his life.

Paul, ever longing to imitate Christ, knew how important it was to invest his life in a small group of people. He taught his disciples everything he knew and wanted them to teach others. We often associate Paul with his correspondence and letters, but his method of making disciples was far more hands-on than most realize. If we take Luke's account in Acts and Paul's writings, he had nineteen traveling companions to help in his missionary journeys over the span of twenty to thirty years. For continuity's sake, those traveling companions are as follows in alphabetical order: Aquilla, Aristarchus, Barnabus, Epaphras, Gaius, Justus, Luke, Marcus, Onesimus, Philemon, Priscilla, Secundus, Silas, Sopater, Tertius, Timothy, Titus, Trophimus, and Tychicus. There were others he counted as coworkers such as Demus, Lydia, and Jason, but even if we added all of them together, there would only be thirty to forty people. In reality, that seems like a small number of individuals to have personal influence over in a ministry spanning three decades, but only because we view disciple-making differently than Jesus and Paul did. Paul, following the example of his master, poured all of his life into only a few people.

Secundus and Aristarchus were both from Thessalonica, traveling with Paul and learning from him what it meant to make disciples. In what we refer to as his second missionary journey, Paul spent a good length of time with the church in Thessalonica, and in his first letter, we get a beautiful picture of Paul's love for the people:

> But we were gentle among you, like a nursing mother taking care of her own children. So, being affectionately desirous of you, we were ready to share with you not only the gospel of God but also our own selves.
>
> —1 Thessalonians 2:7–8

Paul understood what it took to disciple people. He knew it was more than sharing the gospel. He shared his life with them in order to model what it meant to follow Jesus. As the years progressed, he remained with them, investing everything he had in their spiritual development.

Evangelism and Disciple-Making

Growing up, I learned to evangelize the lost. At first, I was trained to know the gospel story and regurgitate it back in a simple way. I first used the "Roman Road," which was a progression of verses in Scripture telling the story of Jesus's sacrifice for our sins. It was simple, to the point, and easy to remember. Through the years, new methods and tools came about. I used jewelry, cubes, t-shirts, colored beads, tapestries, rugs, blankets, videos, drawings on napkins, illustrations, business cards, and even food. They all taught the same thing: Jesus died for your sins, so repent and be saved.

I'm a storyteller at heart, so making presentations of any sort came naturally to me. Over time, I became an expert at declaring the gospel, but no one ever explicitly taught me what to do next. In high school, I would share the gospel with a fellow classmate, ask them to say a prayer, then invite them to church. In retrospect, I never saw any long-term change in people due to my efforts, but somehow, I walked away feeling accomplished.

Looking back, the criteria for gauging success was lacking. Victory hinged on convincing a person to pray for salvation and nothing more. Once the prayer was spoken and the transaction "closed," my responsibility was finished. I loved the exhilarating feeling of sharing the gospel, but there was no follow-through.

For some reason, we've compartmentalized evangelism and disciple-making into two separate things, but we never see that in Scripture. In fact, an equivalent of the word *evangelism* is never found in the Bible. The closest we get is *evangelist*, but that's only in three verses.

And he gave the apostles, the prophets, the evangelists, the shepherds and teachers, to equip the saints for the work of ministry.

—Ephesians 4:11–12

On the next day we departed and came to Caesarea, and we entered the house of Philip the evangelist, who was one of the seven, and stayed with him.

—Acts 21:8

As for you, always be sober-minded, endure suffering, do the work of an evangelist, fulfill your ministry.

—2 Timothy 4:5

The meaning of the Ephesians passage is clear: it's the responsibility of church leadership to train and equip all believers to do the work of the church (go and make disciples). Luke makes it clear that Philip was a leader in the local church, and Paul undoubtedly saw Timothy as someone who was able to teach the good news and lead other believers in the local church. An evangelist is simply someone who "brings good news."

Scripturally speaking, these passages don't build a strong case for evangelism as a spiritual gift. If anything, viewing evangelism as a spiritual gift has damaged the Body of Christ. We've convinced ourselves that only elite Christians can properly express the gospel; however, the whole concept of evangelism is built around the idea of sharing the message and mission of Christ, and that responsibility belongs to all believers.

I know this seems odd, but there's no Greek equivalent for our English word, *evangelism*. We get it from the Greek, *euangelion*, which means "good news," and *euangelizō*, meaning to preach the good news, but we don't translate either as "evangelism" in Scripture. They are translated as "gospel," and "preaching/preaching the gospel," respectively. In other words, we've made two words from one, both with their own distinct meanings.

When most Christians speak of evangelism, they do so with *euangelizō* in mind, meaning the sharing of good news, but not once does Scripture use *euangelizō* in reference to specific gifting of the Spirit to specific men and women. In other words, while the role of an evangelist (*euangelistēs*) is up for discussion, the specific gifting of evangelism (at least how we've come to understand it) does not exist in Scripture.

Thankfully, this connects perfectly with what we know of Jesus's command for all believers to go and make disciples, and herein lies the problem: we have effectively separated the proclamation of the gospel from the follow-through of making disciples. The proclamation of the gospel is not the end goal. The Kingdom of God is the end goal, and that Kingdom requires true disciples.

When Jesus was preaching, he proclaimed the gospel of the Kingdom or the good news of what God wanted to accomplish, and he did this while following through with making disciples. We know God wants to bring himself glory and that gathering worshippers throughout all of history is the major driving force of the Kingdom. Mere proclamation of the gospel apart from making disciples doesn't make sense.

If the end goal is making disciples, then proclaiming the gospel is only the first step. If we preach the gospel but don't make disciples, we're no better than the reluctant prophet, Jonah. He focused on presenting the truth with no follow-through of making disciples. If we continue to think of *evangelism* and disciple-making as separate realities, we will fall into the same trap.

In reality, authentic evangelism creates such a deep passion for new believers that disciple-making should happen naturally. Making disciples organically means this commitment functions as a daily routine. Paul's gospel efforts spurred on his own desire and unmistakable love for the church in Thessalonica. When God changed Paul's life, he effectively changed the lives of everyone Paul would ever meet and disciple. Disciple-making should never end after a believer shares the gospel or invites a nonbeliever to a ministry event. Unfortunately, the ultimate goal of most churches leans toward developing more knowledgeable worshipers, not more mature worshipers. In 1 Thessalonians 2:7–8, Paul confesses to spending a vast amount of time and energy creating and multiplying disciples.

True love argues for a far more hands-on approach than a weekly program or established event. A true disciple-making strategy must start with sharing the good news, but it can't stop there! Too many churches differentiate between evangelism and disciple-making while inadvertently convincing the people in their congregations that the two acts happen separately. In reality, Paul declares in 1 Thessalonians that disciple-making flows from sharing the gospel, and the two should never exist apart from one another.

A focus on the natural flow of disciple-making from preaching, teaching, or sharing the good news of Jesus doesn't mean churches can neglect the believers in their congregations who need discipling. The view of disciple-making seen in Scripture simply fixes a negative, recurring cycle of no follow-through. Sadly, in most of my conversations with believers, they admit to never having had anyone truly disciple them. Someone told them the good news of Jesus and left them to fend for themselves. In contrast, Paul stayed in Thessalonica for an extended time for this very reason. He believed in the idea of "withness," taking the time to share his life instead of preaching a great sermon and leaving the next day.

The idea that two people can connect immediately on an intimate level does not consider the complexity of human nature. Every deep and fulfilling relationship takes time to foster that kind of affinity. Paul understood "withness," and Scripture shows him spending more and more time training and discipling people in the cities he visited. Disciple-making takes time.

It's hard to imagine Paul explaining the complexity of prayer or the spiritual and physical nature of fasting in a short period of time. Spiritual formation requires a focused investment from a more mature believer and the transformative power of the Holy Spirit. Such a change doesn't happen overnight.

Churches have long sent out people from their congregations who are educated about Jesus but don't look or act like him. Following Christ and submitting to his lordship means a transformation takes place. Paul knew that the Thessalonians needed more than an education about the gospel, and he shared his life with them so they could grow as full-fledged ambassadors for Christ.

A specific time set aside every Sunday for a large group gathering will never be the best way to make disciples. Paul gave everything to the Thessalonians. By offering his life, he made himself available and challenged them as he grew in his own relationship with Jesus. Paul surrendered his life to disciple others. There's no such thing as an absent disciple-maker. Our presence is required when we pour Jesus into others. If we want to see true change in people, we have to stick with them. We have to remain dedicated to their spiritual maturity.

Ready, Release, Remain

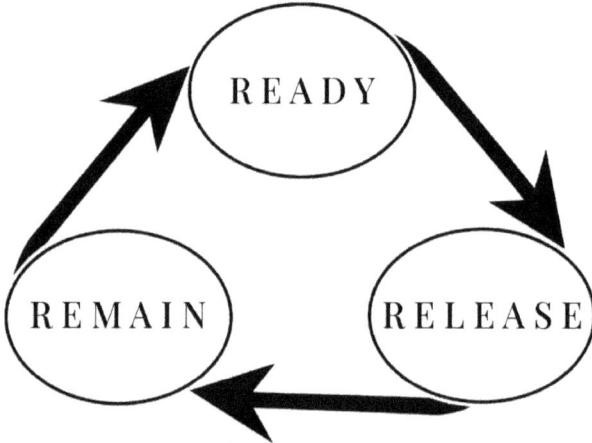

Jesus knew he was training his disciples to change the world, but to change the world, they needed to change first. Jesus taught his disciples so they would effectively become different people who were focused on building his Kingdom instead of satisfying their own desires. After teaching and equipping them to do his work, he sent them out to proclaim his message. When they returned and gave a report to him, the cycle started all over again. He would once again teach them, sometimes encouraging them, but also correcting any wrong behavior. This is how Jesus made disciples. It may seem overly simplistic at first glance, but in reality, it's a lot of hard work. To think we could find a better plan in our day and age is the epitome of arrogance.

Ready

Jesus prepared his disciples to go and make other disciples. When he uttered the Great Commission, there was no question about what Jesus wanted his followers to teach others they came in contact with over the course of their lives. Look closer at what Jesus said in Matthew 28:19–20: "Go therefore and make disciples of all nations, baptizing them in the name of the Father and of the Son and of the Holy Spirit, *teaching them to observe all that I have commanded of you.* And behold, I am with you always, to the end of the age" (emphasis added). Jesus wanted his disciples to teach a very specific set of ideals, those he had laid out throughout his ministry.

Jesus taught in two ways. First, he spoke truth into the lives of his followers. He read Scripture with them and showed how everything came together with one purpose. He taught like a teacher or rabbi would teach his pupils. In other words, there were times when Jesus spoke and the twelve listened to what he had to say. Every word that left his lips was from God, which made it of the utmost importance. What we refer to as the Sermon on the Mount is a great example of teaching through discourse.

> Seeing the crowds, he went up on the mountain, and when he sat down, his disciples came to him. And he opened his mouth and taught them.
>
> —Matthew 5:1–2

For those of us who follow Jesus today, teaching the Word of God to those we disciple is essential. Our words will only get us so far, but Scripture contains the words of life. We must teach and speak what has already been spoken.

As we ready those we disciple to send them out, teaching them about Jesus through reading Scripture is fundamentally important. In God's Word, we find what truly matters. We can only chase after the things of God if we know what they are. We learn about God's design and purpose for our lives in the Bible. Jesus taught his followers what to think, say, and do. We need to take those we disciple and do the same thing by leading them to Scripture.

Second, Jesus was the master of modeling and contextualization in current culture. Think about the time he washed his disciples' feet! That whole story was about modeling and demonstrating a reality for the Kingdom of God.

> Jesus, knowing that the Father had given all things into his hands and that he had come from God and was going back to God, rose from supper. He laid aside his outer garments, and taking a towel, tied it around his waist. Then he poured water into a basin and began to wash the disciples' feet and wipe them with the towel that was wrapped around him. He came to Simon Peter, who said to him, "Lord, do you wash my feet?" Jesus answered him, "What I am doing you do not understand now, but afterward you will understand." Peter said to him, "You shall never wash my feet." Jesus answered him, "If I do not wash you, you have no share with me." Simon Peter said to him, "Lord, not my feet only but also my hands and my head!" Jesus said to him, "The one who has bathed does not need to wash, except for his feet, but is completely clean. And you are clean, but not every one of you." For he knew who was to betray him; that was why he said, "Not all of you are clean."

> When he had washed their feet and put on his outer garments and resumed his place, he said to them, "Do you understand what I have done to you? You call me Teacher and Lord, and you are right, for so I am. If I then, your Lord and Teacher, have washed your feet, you also

ought to wash one another's feet. For I have given you
an example, that you also should do just as I have done
to you. Truly, truly, I say to you, a servant is not greater
than his master, nor is a messenger greater than the one
who sent him. If you know these things, blessed are you
if you do them."

—John 13:3–17

Jesus wasn't teaching his disciples how to wash feet. In
fact, it bares importance that we never read of the disciples
washing feet in Scripture after this moment! This doesn't
mean the disciples were disobedient, but it might mean we've
misunderstood what Jesus was trying to teach them. He was
showing them how to impact the world by laying down their
lives for others. Jesus came to give his life as a ransom, and this
was just another way to show what it meant to sacrifice your
life for another.

Jesus was the master of object lessons. Most of the time, his
disciples learned what was important by watching him interact
with others. Remaining with the people we disciple means we
get the chance to live out the gospel right before their eyes.

Readying and equipping the people you disciple is also
where spiritual disciplines come into play. The longer we stay
with our disciples, the more opportunity we have to help them
grow in Christlikeness. Through word and action, we can teach
with a specific goal in mind.

Have nothing to do with irreverent, silly myths. Rather
train yourself for godliness; for while bodily training is of
some value, godliness is of value in every way, as it holds
promise for the present life and also for the life to come.

—1 Timothy 4:7–8

The goal is godliness. Spiritual disciplines without the goal of Christlikeness are devoid of any value. Jesus taught his disciples about practices that would allow them to grow in their faith. He modeled how to pray, worship, memorize Scripture, and even how to get away from the crowds and spend time with his Heavenly Father.

Peter learned to teach and model Scripture to those he discipled. He knew the people he invested his life in had to work hard to grow in their faith, so he encouraged them to be diligent as they pursued Jesus. In his first letter, we get a beautiful picture of what spiritual investment looks like in disciple-making.

> Therefore I intend always to remind you of these qualities, though you know them and are established in the truth that you have. I think it right, as long as I am in this body, to stir you up by way of reminder, since I know that the putting off of my body will be soon, as our Lord Jesus Christ made clear to me. And I will make every effort so that after my departure you may be able at any time to recall these things.
>
> —2 Peter 1:12–15

Peter wanted to "make every effort" while he was here on this earth to prepare and ready his disciples to follow Jesus. Teaching people to obey the things of Christ is a full-time responsibility most believers don't take seriously, but if we want to make disciples, we have to teach them. We have to lead them and model for them what Jesus taught his own disciples during his ministry on earth.

Release

Learning a skill and never using it makes no sense in the grand scheme of things. If I spent most of my life learning how to fix cars and then never actually fixed a car, it would all be devoid of any value. Likewise, training and equipping people to be disciples of Jesus and never intentionally releasing them to do the same would void any and all effort to help them think, speak and act more like Jesus. Learning about Jesus is useless unless that knowledge is put into action. Jesus made disciples, and he told us to go and do the same thing. We must release the people we disciple so they can fulfill the Great Commission. It's the reason we make disciples in the first place.

There are stories of Jesus releasing his followers to go and make disciples before the Great Commission. He was training them even before he commissioned them. Releasing those we disciple is part of the process.

> And he called the twelve together and gave them power and authority over all demons and to cure diseases, and he sent them out to proclaim the kingdom of God and to heal. And he said to them, "Take nothing for your journey, no staff, nor bag, nor bread, nor money; and do not have two tunics. And whatever house you enter, stay there, and from there depart. And wherever they do not receive you, when you leave that town shake off the dust from your feet as a testimony against them." And they departed and went through the villages, preaching the gospel and healing everywhere.
>
> —Luke 9:1–6

Matthew gives us another version of this story in his Gospel. He emphasizes the overwhelming nature of what Jesus was calling them to do. Our Savior knew his followers would be persecuted in the process of advancing the Kingdom.

> These twelve Jesus sent out, instructing them, "Go nowhere among the Gentiles and enter no town of the Samaritans but go rather to the lost sheep of the house of Israel. And proclaim as you go, saying, 'The kingdom of heaven is at hand.' Heal the sick, raise the dead, cleanse lepers, cast out demons. You received without paying; give without pay. Acquire no gold or silver or copper for your belts, no bag for your journey, or two tunics or sandals or a staff, for the laborer deserves his food. And whatever town or village you enter, find out who is worthy in it and stay there until you depart. As you enter the house, greet it. And if the house is worthy, let your peace come upon it, but if it is not worthy, let your peace return to you. And if anyone will not receive you or listen to your words, shake off the dust from your feet when you leave that house or town. Truly, I say to you, it will be more bearable on the day of judgment for the land of Sodom and Gomorrah than for that town.

> Behold, I am sending you out as sheep among wolves, so be wise as serpents and innocent as doves. Beware of men, for they will deliver you over to courts and flog you in their synagogues, and you will be dragged before governors and kings for my sake, to bear witness before them and the Gentiles. When they deliver you over, do not be anxious how you are to speak or what you are to say, for what you are to say will be given to you in that hour. For it is not you who speak, but the Spirit of your Father speaking through you. Brother will deliver brother over to death, and the father his child, and children will

rise against parents and have them put to death, and you will be hated by all for my name's sake. But the one who endures to the end will be saved. When they persecute you in one town, flee to the next, for truly, I say to you, you will not have gone through all the towns of Israel before the Son of Man comes."

—Matthew 10:5–23

Jesus purposefully sent out his disciples, and this wasn't the only time he entrusted such an important task to them. If anything, their responsibility to proclaim the gospel only grew from here. Jesus was quickly releasing them into the world to do his work and make disciples. We must be intentional in sending out those whom we disciple. We are training them to do with others what we are doing with them.

Remain

Jesus always followed up with his disciples after their life experiences. He knew every moment spent proclaiming the gospel was also an opportunity to grow in their faith. When the people we invest in are released to go and make disciples, our responsibility to continue discipling them remains crucial to their spiritual development. Jesus released his followers, only to have them come back and report on their work. By choosing to remain close to those he discipled, Jesus opened the door for continual growth. Disciple-making is a lifelong process.

After this, the Lord appointed seventy-two others and sent them on ahead of him, two by two, into every town and place where he was about to go. And he said to them, "The harvest is plentiful, but the laborers are few. Therefore pray earnestly to the Lord of the harvest to send out laborers into his harvest. Go your way; behold, I am sending you out as lambs in the midst of wolves. Carry no moneybag, no knapsack, no sandals, and greet no one on the road. Whatever house you enter, first say, 'Peace be to this house!' And if a son of peace is there, your peace will rest upon him. But if not, it will return to you. And remain in the same house, eating and drinking what they provide, for the laborer deserves his wages. Do not go from house to house. Whenever you enter a town and they receive you, eat what is set before you. Heal the sick in it and say to them, 'The kingdom of God has come near to you.' But whenever you enter a town and they do not receive you, go into its streets and say, 'Even the dust of your town that clings to our feet we wipe off against you. Nevertheless know this, that the kingdom of God has come near.' I tell you, it will be more bearable on that day for Sodom than for that town.

"Woe to you, Chorazin! Woe to you, Bethsaida! For if the mighty works done in you had been done in Tyre and Sidon, they would have repented long ago, sitting in sackcloth and ashes. But it will be more bearable in the judgment for Tyre and Sidon than for you. And you, Capernaum, will you be exalted to heaven? You shall be brought down to Hades. The one who hears you hears me, and the one who rejects you rejects me, and the one who rejects me rejects him who sent me."

The seventy two returned with joy, saying, "Lord, even the demons are subject to us in your name!" And he said to them, "I saw Satan fall like lightning from heaven. Behold, I have given you authority to tread on serpents and scorpions, and over all the power of the enemy, and nothing shall hurt you. Nevertheless, do not rejoice in this, that the spirits are subject to you, but rejoice that your names are written in heaven."

—Luke 10:1–20

When we remain with our disciples, it allows for the discipling relationship to continue instead of coming to an abrupt end. It allows for teachable and re-teachable moments. All of this continues to foster a feeling of unity of purpose and mind between the discipler and the disciple. Jesus turned a moment of celebration into another chance to teach his disciples about rejection, sin, repentance, and their own salvation. Paul and Timothy also shared a similar relationship.

For this reason, when I could bear it no longer, I sent to learn about your faith, for fear that somehow the tempter had tempted you and our labor would be in vain. But now that Timothy has come to us from you, and has brought us the good news of your faith and love and reported that you always remember us kindly and long to see us, as we long to see you—for this reason, brothers, in all our distress and affliction we have been comforted about you through your faith.

—1 Thessalonians 3:5–7

Timothy, a disciple of Paul, was reporting on his disciple-making efforts after Paul had released him to Thessalonica. Reporting leads to readying, which again leads to the release of disciples to make even more disciples. The cycle doesn't have to end, and it should persist as long as God allows. Remaining with those we disciple is the essence of "withness." We choose to stay with them for the benefit of their spiritual growth.

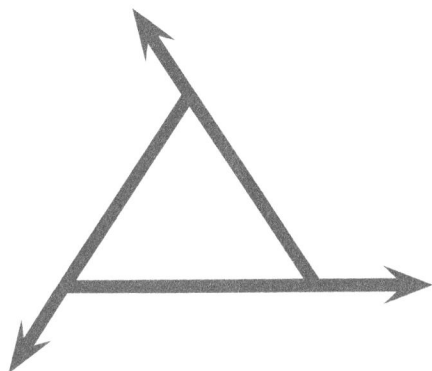

CHAPTER EIGHT

Domain

The Beauty of the Church in Rome

I love the book of Romans. It contains some of the greatest passages in Scripture. As a pastor, I know I'm supposed to love all Scripture (don't worry, I do), but the beauty of this letter gets me every time. I would love to tackle the entirety of Romans in this book, but far greater men than me have done so in commentary form. What I really want to address is the story behind the church in Rome. From a human standpoint, it's magnificently baffling how it came about.

From what limited information we have, we know that the birth of the church in Rome didn't match our modern church-planting efforts. Today, when people or organizations plant, they sometimes pinpoint an area considered unchurched. Other times, people plant because they know a church will be successful in a growing area. Rome was nothing like that.

No one fully knows how the church started. Luke states in Acts 2:10 that there were "visitors from Rome" at Pentecost, but that's really all we have to go on. What we do know is that Christianity spread so fast and anchored so deep that Emperor Claudius expelled all believers from Rome in the early days of the Church. Only after he died did the Christians come back to the city. In the book of Romans, Paul writes to those believers who returned after the death of Claudius.

How did Christianity spread to Rome so fast? Paul had never been there. He was a Roman citizen, but he had never visited Rome. We can logically conclude that the church in Rome didn't begin because the disciples sent a church planter to set up shop. We have no record of any such efforts. Most likely, it existed because new believers returned home from Pentecost and started living out their new lives with Jesus. It happened because loving Jesus was a part of their everyday lives. A church was established because Christians were there, not because they were sent there by anyone in particular.

Domains are where people spend the majority of their time and have a certain amount of influence. For the Romans who went to Pentecost, Rome was their domain. It's where they resided, so it made sense to build God's Kingdom where he had placed them. Imagine what would happen if all believers treated their domains as their disciple-making grounds instead of limiting their efforts to the local church once a week. We would get something similar to the church in Rome: an organic form of disciple-making, fueled by the belief that all Christians are disciple-makers and Kingdom builders. We would get what Jesus intended.

What Is My Domain?

Simply put, your domain is where you spend most of your time and where you have a certain amount of influence. For most people, this falls into two categories: work/school and home. However, those are by no means the only two domains.

For students, it could be an extracurricular activity or club. Stay-at-home moms have their families, but they could also be part of a co-op of some kind or a playgroup. As far as domains go, the possibilities are endless, but it's important to understand something: the only people who have a local church as their domain are the people who work there. This doesn't exclude them from making disciples. If anything, it means they have to work even harder to make sure they go into the world and seek out other domains. The temptation to stay inside the church walls is great, even for pastors.

Why Domains?

Growing up the son of a Southern Baptist pastor means I got to observe all types of things in the church. I got to see the breadth of human emotion, the depth of human depravity, and the majesty of everything God can accomplish in and through his children. It also meant that much of my life was bogged down with well-meaning and well-intentioned people who had been institutionalized instead of transformed and restored. Going to church was the southern thing to do, which meant that any good ole boy from Texas was there on Sunday morning. It wasn't who we were necessarily. It was just what we did. So often the true nature of our spirituality was marginalized by our traditions.

The church was where we went to learn about God and hear a sermon. We threw around the word *discipleship* every now and again, and in my later years of ministry, we even started using it to describe pastoral positions in the church. "Education Pastor" just didn't have the same hipness as "Pastor of Discipleship." The problem is the job description never really changed. As much as we wanted to make disciples, we ended up with passive attendees, educated people who could show up and experience community, but never really live out what it meant to be a disciple or make disciples.

Volunteering your time and services at church became the expected norm instead of taking the gospel to the ends of the earth. We might remember our Sunday School teachers fondly (some of us even owe our spiritual lives to them), but we only saw them once a week. They made the Bible come alive to us, but it mostly added up to a bunch of thematically connected stories we stored in the deepest recesses of our brains. The goal was never to walk and talk with us daily like Jesus did with his disciples. We weren't taught to live that way.

Christianity exploded in Rome because normal people took the gospel everywhere. They took it to their homes, places of work, and the cultural hot spots of the day. If this wasn't the case, then Claudius's expulsion of all believers doesn't make sense. The gospel made such a quick and substantial impact in Rome that it turned the emperor's world upside down.

If we expect to do the same and turn the world upside down for the Kingdom of God, then all believers must learn to take the gospel and share it in their domains. Time is everything when making disciples. Domains make sense because time is of the essence, and making disciples will take every bit of time we can spare.

Most believers see the potential time it takes to build the Kingdom and run away from their God-given purpose in life. The easy thing to do in churches is just show up and listen. The uncomfortable thing to do is volunteer in a classroom or small group, but the extremely difficult task is making disciples. It takes your entire life and everything you are, and most of it takes place outside the local church.

Jesus knew the moments he spent with his disciples were precious. He had a limited amount of time to train and equip them to change the world, which meant even the smallest comforts were sacrificed in order to make the biggest impact. Disciples, by their very nature, are needy people, and that's not a bad thing.

> One day he got into a boat with his disciples, and he said to them, "Let us go across to the other side of the lake." So they set out, and as they sailed he fell asleep. And a windstorm came down on the lake, and they were filling with water and were in danger. And they went and woke him, saying, "Master, Master, we are perishing!" And he awoke and rebuked the wind and the raging waves, and they ceased, and there was a calm. He said to them, "Where is your faith?" And they were afraid, and they marveled, saying to one another, "Who then is this, that he commands even winds and water, and they obey him?"
>
> —Luke 8:22–25

Jesus was with his disciples almost every day for three years. He was at their constant beck and call no matter what time of day. Yes, he took time for himself, but more often than not, his disciples were still looking for him while he tried to steal some very important alone time with his Heavenly Father. The disciples were his spiritual children and his eternal legacy. They required his time and attention, even if it meant messing up a much-needed nap.

Domains make sense because you can begin discipling relationships right where you are. Contrary to what we've been told, the gospel belongs everywhere. Places of work now become places of worship where we can see the Holy Spirit transform the lives of others. Schools finally become the mission grounds they were supposed to be instead of being a pool of kids we draft our top picks to grow our youth groups. We engage domains by making disciples in those places.

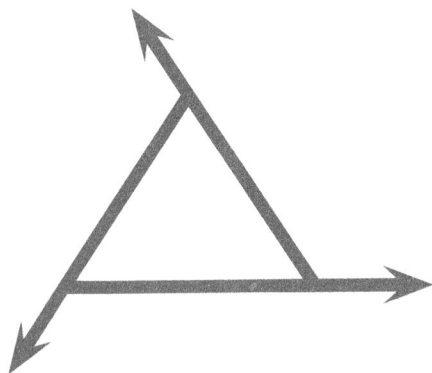

CHAPTER NINE

The Measure of a Man

The Difficult Task of Measurement

Growing up in the modern church, you hear a lot about the "health" of a local body. Everyone has their own opinion on what makes a healthy church, but two measurements stick out more than others in conversations with pastors and others in ministry: attendance and the number of salvations/baptisms. Pastors either love or hate the conversation.

Pastors of large churches tend to love the conversation because it paints their church in a healthy limelight, while all too often it's possible for pastors of smaller churches to feel inferior in their endeavors. In fact, when these two measurements come up, you tend to hear phrases like, "Well that church is in a difficult area," or "That's a really good number for that size of church." I can't stress with enough vigor how unhealthy these conversations have been in my own life and in the life of churches I've been involved with on some level.

But what about baptisms? Don't baptisms measure the health of a growing and thriving church by showing the number of new Christians? Maybe, but that number can also be deceiving. While new converts are important, they can't guarantee a healthy church. I've been in contact with many churches that baptize a lot of people but have nothing to show for it. Baptisms are extremely important, but they don't measure the overall health of a local church. The same can be said for Sunday morning attendance. As painful as it is to admit for most pastors (including myself), all of this can be manipulated and misinterpreted. All of it can be one massive distraction.

Quantitative Measurements

Quantitative measurements are those that focus on the completion of tasks or the number of tasks completed. Without getting too ridiculous in our efforts to name all the things that churches measure from a quantifiable standpoint, here are a few of the most common ones:

- Number of baptisms

- Attendance

- The accomplishment of spiritual disciplines

- Confession (for all my Roman Catholic brothers and sisters)

- Number of small groups

The list could go on, but I think you probably get the idea.

Should we use quantitative measurements? Sure, you can. I do to an extent, but I never want to fall into the trap of believing they give an accurate representation of the church at large. You should always look at any quantifiable measurement with a keen eye set on the dangers that come with it. With quantitative measurements, the temptation to believe the hype is never far behind.

Qualitative Measurements

Qualitative measurements, to get right to the point, are the measurements Jesus took to heart. They are the things that help us look, think, speak, and act more like Jesus. I know we use that terminology a lot, but it's true. That's the goal of disciple-making. God always cares more about the qualitative nature of a person rather than their quantifiable achievements. Take a look at what God says to Samuel when Israel was looking for a king:

> When they came, he looked on Eliab and thought, "Surely the Lord's anointed is before him." But the Lord said to Samuel, "Do not look on his appearance or on the height of his stature, because I have rejected him. For the Lord sees not as man sees: man looks on the outward appearance, but the Lord looks on the heart."
>
> —1 Samuel 16:6–7

Jeremiah was a prophet who knew he couldn't hide anything from God. He knew God cared about the qualitative side of things: "But you, O Lord, know me; you see me, and test my heart toward you" (Jeremiah 12:3).

There's a heart issue we'll never be able to measure through quantitative methods. The size of a person's heart doesn't measure their ability to love people, just like showing up at a church service doesn't truly measure your love for Jesus. In other words, our churches are potentially full of people who've been living quantifiable "Christian" lives instead of qualitative lives of obedience.

God tells us in his Word what matters to him. We see his character and desires in the person of Jesus, and the Holy Spirit works in our lives to mend what sin has broken. God is clear about what he loves and how he wants his children to live.

> But I say, walk by the Spirit, and you will not gratify the desires of the flesh. For the desires of the flesh are against the Spirit, and the desires of the Spirit are against the flesh, for these are opposed to each other, to keep you from doing the things you want to do. But if you are led by the Spirit, you are not under the law. Now the works of the flesh are evident: sexual immorality, impurity, sensuality, idolatry, sorcery, enmity, strife, jealousy, fits of anger, rivalries, dissensions, divisions, envy, drunkenness, orgies, and things like these. I warn you, as I warned you before, that those who do such things will not inherit the kingdom of God. But the fruit of the Spirit is love, joy, peace, patience, kindness, goodness, faithfulness, gentleness, self-control; against such things there is no law.
>
> —Galatians 5:16–23

The fruit of the Spirit allows us to see what God desires in the hearts of all his children. In fact, it's clear throughout Scripture that these are the attributes the Spirit grows in those who are faithfully seeking God the Father. Let's list them:

- Love
- Joy
- Peace
- Patience

- Kindness
- Goodness
- Faithfulness
- Gentleness
- Self-Control

Most people would say these things are abstract, and therefore, unmeasurable, but that's a shallow view of the Holy Spirit's power to change people. Let's take a look at one more passage before tackling the "how" of measuring these qualities. In his first letter to the church in Corinth, Paul speaks of what should be defining characteristics of all believers.

If I speak in the tongues of men and of angels, but have not love, I am a noisy gong or a clanging cymbal. And if I have prophetic powers, and understand all mysteries and all knowledge, and if I have all faith, so as to remove mountains, but have not love, I am nothing. If I give away all I have, and if I deliver up my body to be burned, but have not love, I gain nothing.

Love is patient and kind; love does not envy or boast; it is not arrogant or rude. It does not insist on its own way; it is not irritable or resentful; it does not rejoice at wrongdoing, but rejoices with the truth. Love bears all things, believes all things, hopes all things, endures all things.

Love never ends. As for prophecies, they will pass away; as for tongues, they will cease; as for knowledge, it will pass away. For we know in part and we prophesy in part, but when the perfect comes, the partial will pass away. When I was a child, I spoke like a child, I thought like a child, I reasoned like a child. When I became a man,

I gave up childish ways. For now we see in a mirror dimly, but then face to face. Now I know in part; then I shall know fully, even as I have been fully known.

So now faith, hope, and love abide, these three; but the greatest of these is love.

—1 Corinthians 13:1–13

Faith, hope, and love are three things in which every believer should grow as they walk with God. Believers also need to focus on these qualities as they disciple others. Unfortunately, people don't want to do the hard work of disciple-making because measuring the quality of each disciple takes time and energy. Herein lies the power of *remaining* with those we disciple. As we pour our lives into others, it's impossible to measure the growth of these qualities unless we're intimately involved in their lives.

Remain – How to Measure the Immeasurable

Jesus knew his disciples intimately. He knew them because he spent time with them, remaining a big part of their lives. He knew where they were spiritually and where they needed to go. He knew the progression of each individual because he dared to stay with them and put in the time necessary to make disciples. Jesus stayed with his followers, even when they didn't deserve it. After Peter denied Jesus, all could have been lost. Jesus had every right to walk away and deny Peter in return. Instead, he stayed with Peter, refusing to leave him during his pain.

When they had finished breakfast, Jesus said to Simon Peter, "Simon, son of John, do you love me more than

these?" He said to him, "Yes, Lord; you know that I love
you." He said to him, "Feed my lambs." He said to him
a second time, "Simon, son of John, do you love me?"
He said to him, "Yes, Lord; you know that I love you."
He said to him, "Tend my sheep." He said to him the
third time, "Simon, son of John, do you love me?" Peter
was grieved because he said to him the third time, "Do
you love me?" and he said to him, "Lord, you know
everything; you know that I love you." Jesus said to him,
"Feed my sheep."

—John 21:15–17

To disciple someone is to know them. To know them is to
remain with them. It's possible to measure a disciple from a
qualitative standpoint, but only if you know and understand
them. You learn to know them and where they are in their
spiritual lives through daily interactions. This is why making
disciples in your domain makes so much sense. I know the
young men I disciple. I know where they are in their walks with
God, and that allows me to speak about their current situations.
In order to make disciples, we have to lay down our lives to be
with them.

"This is my commandment, that you love one another
as I have loved you. Greater love has no one than this,
that someone lay down his life for his friends. You are
my friends if you do what I command you. No longer do
I call you servants, for the servant does not know what his
master is doing; but I have called you friends, for all that
I have heard from my Father I have made known to you.
You did not choose me, but I chose you and appointed
you that you should go and bear fruit and that your fruit
should abide, so that whatever you ask the Father in my

name, he may give it to you. These things I command
you, so that you will love one another."

—John 15:12–17

We must remember that this interaction between Jesus and
his disciples occurred *before his death*, so the phrase "lay down
his life for his friends" must have been in reference to what
had already taken place. Jesus had given the disciples every
part of himself. Every day that he taught, listened to, corrected,
equipped, and loved was necessary to grow them into godly men
who would change the world. Jesus understood his disciples
and what they needed because he remained with them, laying
down his life so they could know God better. His death saved
them, but his life discipled them.

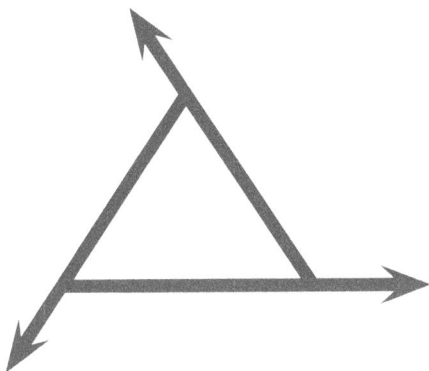

CHAPTER TEN

The Word of God

What We've Lost

Ministry of any type always provides opportunities for interesting conversations. Most of the time, people approach pastors for advice on certain subjects. Counseling sessions often turn into, "please tell me what to do" sessions, or even worse, "please tell me what I'm doing is right" scenarios. No matter what the situation, most people are looking for confirmation of what they already feel to be right in their own hearts. Unfortunately, our hearts are ultimately self-centered, even when we start with the best intentions.

> The heart is deceitful above all things, and desperately sick; who can understand it? "I the Lord search the heart and test the mind, to give every man according to his ways, according to the fruit of his deeds."
>
> —Jeremiah 17:9–10

In the corruptness of our sin, we have lost the ability to think with the mind of Christ. If we can't reason effectively because of our own wickedness, we need something to keep us on track. If we don't have a way to measure our thoughts and feelings, we're left paralyzed by our own sin and unrighteousness.

> In those days there was no king in Israel. Everyone did what was right in his own eyes.
>
> —Judges 17:6

Everyone has their own agenda, and we instinctively want to elevate ourselves above all others. No one is above temptation, so we need something to help us evaluate our thoughts and actions. In his grace and mercy, God has given us his Word, and everything should be measured by Scripture.

I remember a conversation with a young woman who was convinced it was God's will for her to commit suicide. After asking her how she came to such a conclusion, she responded by telling me she had prayed about it and received confirmation from God himself. As crazy as it sounds, that's how most of us treat God's will in our lives. We measure his will against our own desires. It never crosses our minds to evaluate what we think by seeking truth in the Word of God. We simply hope God thinks like us.

This is what we've lost. We've lost our love for God's Word. It's just easier to assume we know what God would do in a certain situation, but as disciples of Jesus, we must know his heart before we can imitate his actions or take part in his mission. Scripture clearly illustrates the heart of God, and as his ambassadors, we must know what it says to teach those we disciple. Sadly, too many believers are not taught how to study God's Word. Instead, we're content to be told what it says, paying attention to what we like and dismissing what we don't as outdated and inapplicable.

When it comes to making disciples, Scripture is the most important tool we have in helping others look, think, and act like Jesus. We don't have to reason, guess, or infer how God feels about anything. His Word speaks directly to whatever circumstances or situations we are currently experiencing.

In my conversations with others, when I ask them about issues of purpose or morality, they will eventually utter the phrase, "I feel." There are other variations of this phrase, such as, "I believe," "I think," "I know in my heart," or any number of expressions with an egocentric bent.

Scripture teaches us that our ability to discern and judge (without the Word of God and illumination from the Holy Spirit) is severely lacking. Our hearts are deceitful, and our motives are suspect. Even when we sincerely believe our thoughts and actions are pure, we need something that acts as a litmus test of sorts. Scripture is the litmus test by which we must examine all things. It's how we test our hearts, motives, and actions in a world where everyone is fighting for their own legitimacy.

With disciple-making, Scripture is key to our own growth, as well as the growth of those we disciple. When the young men I teach and equip come with questions, we immediately go to God's Word and see what he has to say about the subject. It doesn't matter what I think or how I feel. I'm not teaching them to think like me. I want them to imitate Christ and no one else. Culture may drive each generation to value different things, but God never changes. Scripture teaches us about an unchanging God with an unwavering mission. For this reason alone, we must learn how to read it correctly and teach those we disciple to do the same.

Studying and Teaching Others

You can find many great resources that will lead you through a Bible study. You can always find a book or lesson to study God's Word, but what most believers are missing is the ability to study on their own. Let's face it: we're as individualistic as they come. We're selfish and egocentric, and sadly this affects the way we read Scripture. We want to read it to see what it says about us. That's why the most common question after reading Scripture is, "What does this mean to you?" That's a horrible question to start with! You aren't the main character in the Bible. This isn't your story, and you're not the hero.

Scripture is God's big story. It's all about him, so to ask what his words mean to me is a little self-absorbed if you really think about it. If I continue to ask what it means to me, then I set myself up to be a chief manipulator of Scripture when applying it to my life. Another possibility is ignoring books, chapters, or verses we consider to be "hard" passages in Scripture. If it's all about what it means to me, then I'm tempted to stick to the passages I like and ignore the ones I don't. To avoid these pitfalls, we want to ask three questions when reading and studying any passage of Scripture:

1. What does this Scripture say about God?
2. What does this Scripture say about God's world?
3. What does this Scripture say about God's church/ people?

A Closer Look at Proverbs 1:1–7

As we discuss what it means to really read and study God's Word, let's take a look at a specific passage and use our three questions to dive a little deeper. The book of Proverbs is a fascinating read. Obviously, wisdom is pretty important considering Scripture tells us it comes from God, so let's take a look at Proverbs 1:1–7:

> The proverbs of Solomon, son of David, king of Israel: To know wisdom and instruction, to understand words of insight, to receive instruction in wise dealing, in righteousness, justice, and equity; to give prudence to the simple, knowledge and discretion to the youth—Let the wise hear and increase in learning, and the one who understands obtain guidance, to understand a proverb and a saying, the words of the wise and their riddles. The fear of the Lord is the beginning of knowledge; fools despise wisdom and instruction.

What Does This Scripture Say About God?

The entirety of Scripture says something about God. This is his story, and he has laid it out for all to hear. If you ever find a verse and think it has nothing to do with God, then you're not reading it in a broad enough context. All Scripture first and foremost points to an all-powerful God. He is the protagonist of the story.

In this Proverbs passage, God is full of wisdom. In fact, he is the ultimate source of wisdom and has made his wisdom manifest in Jesus. There is no wisdom apart from him and anything in human form pretending to have wisdom is a farce.

What Does This Scripture Say About God's World?

This is still God's world. He created it and gave everything its own purpose. Sometimes, Scripture specifically gives us an insight into the complexity of this world and the damage sin has done to God's perfect creation. The state of the real world will always point to the need for a perfect God.

In this passage, the world is absent of wisdom. Apart from God, the world is lost and has no hope. The world despises true wisdom and instruction because it wants to have control and a say over what is true.

What Does This Scripture Say About God's Church/People?

Scripture has one meaning for all people. It doesn't mean something different for each individual. God purposefully and specifically said what he wanted and needed to say. The universal application of Scripture is important in disciple-making.

In the Proverbs passage above, we learn that the Church and humanity are embodied by the idea of choice. There is potential for the world to know wisdom through the grace of God, and that's what the Church should strive for every day. God has chosen his Church and the Church can choose to seek after God. Fools may despise the wisdom and instruction that comes from the Lord, but the Church must rely on it. After all, the fear of the Lord is the beginning of knowledge.

What Next?

The reading and studying of Scripture have no power unless we apply it to our lives. Appreciation does not equal transformation. The whole point of studying Scripture is to become more like Jesus, allowing the Holy Spirit to restore the Imago Dei in us. Reading the Word of God and doing nothing is disobedience. If we do nothing, we're like the lazy servant in the Parable of the Talents.

> For it will be like a man going on a journey, who called his servants and entrusted to them his property. To one

he gave five talents, to another two, to another one, to each according to his ability. Then he went away. He who had received the five talents went at once and traded with them, and he made five talents more. So also he who had the two talents made two talents more. But he who had received the one talent went and dug in the ground and hid his master's money. Now after a long time, the master of those servants came and settled accounts with them. And he who had received the five talents came forward, bringing five talents more, saying, 'Master, you delivered to me five talents; here I have made five talents more.' His master said to him, 'Well done, good and faithful servant. You have been faithful over a little; I will set you over much. Enter into the joy of your master.' And he also who had the two talents came forward, saying, 'Master, you delivered to me two talents; here I have made two talents more.' His master said to him, 'Well done, good and faithful servant. You have been faithful over a little; I will set you over much. Enter into the joy of your master.' He also who had received the one talent came forward, saying, 'Master, I knew you to be a hard man, reaping where you did not sow, and gathering where you scattered no seed, so I was afraid, and I went and hid your talent in the ground. Here you have what is yours.' But his master answered him, 'You wicked and slothful servant! You knew that I reap where I have not sown and gather where I scattered no seed? Then you ought to have invested my money with the bankers, and at my coming I should have received what was my own with interest. So take the talent from him and give it to him who has the ten talents. For to everyone who has will more be given, and he will have an abundance. But from the one who has not, even what he has will be taken away. And cast the worthless servant into the outer darkness. In that place there will be weeping and gnashing of teeth.'

—Matthew 25:14–30

We can't call ourselves followers of Jesus if we do nothing. Following Jesus means obeying his commandments, and by studying his Word, we can know his heart. We can't be disciples (or make disciples) if we don't know his story, but if we know his story and refuse to advance the Kingdom, we're merely observers, not followers. Once we've properly read the Scripture, we need to take action. Once again, there is no transformation without application, and here are three questions to instigate a Gospel response:

1. What do I do now that I know the character of God better?

2. What does this mean for the people I disciple?

3. How do I equip them to live in this truth?

What Do I Do Now That I Know the Character of God Better?

Scripture isn't the disjointed ramblings of fallible human beings. The Word of God is a cohesive story, told through the leading of the Holy Spirit by faithful followers of Yahweh. This is God's story. He initiated everything, so Scripture is about him. If we understand the character of God better after reading it, then it should change the way we live.

In Proverbs 1:1–7, we learn that God is full of wisdom. If God is the only source of true wisdom, then we should follow his leading and nothing else. In fact, all other "wisdom" is inferior to what we see from God in Scripture.

What Does This Mean for the People I Disciple?

If we learn something in Scripture, it makes sense to pass on the wisdom we find to those we disciple. There is a direct correlation between what we read and what we teach to others (which is why reading the entirety of Scripture is so important). We have no wisdom of our own to match what is revealed to us in the Word of God.

From the Proverbs passage, we learn that God is the source of all wisdom. As disciple-makers, there is always the temptation to give advice based on what we feel instead of what we see in Scripture, but that must never be allowed. The only good thing you have to teach your disciples is whatever the Holy Spirit has revealed to us in the Bible. Everything else is based on human effort and understanding.

How Do I Equip Them to Live in This Truth?

Once again, we remember Jesus spent time with his disciples, teaching them, releasing them for Kingdom work, and remaining with them as they grew in faith. If we read Scripture and do nothing, then our reading is in vain. The same applies to those we disciple. Teaching them to live an active faith that changes in light of Scripture is of vast importance.

If Proverbs 1:1–7 teaches us that all wisdom comes from God, we must make sure we are only teaching those we disciple to seek answers from Scripture. This also applies to anyone our own disciples end up discipling. Teaching them to rely on the wisdom of God means they should only teach Scripture as well. We can't match the wisdom of God, so we must rely on what he has given us.

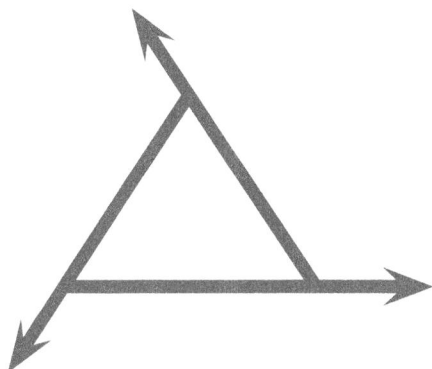

CHAPTER ELEVEN

To What End?

And Jesus came and said to them, "All authority in heaven and on earth has been given to me. Go therefore and make disciples of all nations, baptizing them in the name of the Father and of the Son and of the Holy Spirit, teaching them to observe all that I have commanded you. And behold, I am with you always, to the end of the age."

—Matthew 28:18–20

The Responsibility of Every Believer

As a young pastor, I didn't understand how to deal with the daily grind of ministry, and the position came with a huge amount of influence and power. This caused two things to happen. First, I bought into the idea that I was a lot wiser than I actually was. Second, I grew to like the attention. After a lot of mistakes (some of them the biggest of my life so far), I finally realized that our view of church leadership is flawed.

Pastors are seen as elite Christians who have everything together. Believers have a false and undeserved view of their pastors, and this misconception puts people in leadership at a disadvantage. I remember feeling like everyone was watching me, and I didn't want to mess up. If I was struggling with something, I kept it to myself because I truly believed no one wanted a frail and vulnerable pastor.

This misunderstanding of the pastoral role has caused a lot of problems. First, it creates an environment in which the Body of Christ is focused on the ability of a few individuals to wow a crowd with their deep understanding of Scripture (or maybe they just tell really good stories). I wish the era of the "rock-star" pastor was on its way out, but it always seems to go in cycles. If you think I'm picking on a few pastors because they have large congregations, I promise I'm not doing anything of the sort. Unfortunately, the tendency to treat pastors like rock stars is a sickness that pervades all denominations and all different-sized churches. There are positive exceptions: One of the greatest and most humble pastors I know shepherds one of the largest congregations in Texas.

Second, popular misconceptions convince the majority of the congregation that pastors are the elite evangelists and disciple-makers of the church. As a result, members rely on their pastors to engage in the work Jesus meant for all believers while they comfortably observe from afar. Pastors share the gospel at evangelistic events, people come to Christ, and everyone stands in awe of how effective the speaker was in communicating the plan of salvation. In this scenario, even the most devout Christians often marvel at how God worked through one individual while being completely unaware that God wants to use them in the same manner.

Pastors are not the main disciple-makers in a church. In fact, there is no such thing as a "main" disciple-maker. Pastors do have a specific role to play in the life of a local church, but that doesn't exclude everyone else from their God-given purpose. Read what Paul says about church leaders and their responsibility to all believers.

> And he gave the apostles, the prophets, the evangelists, the shepherds, and teachers, to equip the saints for the work of ministry, for building up the body of Christ, until we all attain to the unity of the faith and of the knowledge of the Son of God, to mature manhood, to the measure of the stature of the fullness of Christ, so that we may no longer be children, tossed to and fro by the waves and carried about by every wind of doctrine, by human cunning, by craftiness in deceitful schemes. Rather, speaking the truth in love, we are to grow up in every way into him who is the head, into Christ, from whom the whole body, joined and held together by every joint with which it is equipped, when each part is working properly, makes the body grow so that it builds itself up in love.
>
> —Ephesians 4:11–16

This passage is about being and making disciples. The role of the pastor is to equip believers in the congregation to go and do the work of the Church (which is to make disciples). It is the responsibility of all believers to advance the Kingdom of God by making disciples. In other words, if you are not making disciples, you are outside of God's will for your life and denying the purpose of your existence. Every believer is a disciple. Every disciple is a disciple-maker, which makes them Kingdom builders.

Be the Few

It's a sobering reminder when we observe just how few people responded in faith while Jesus walked this earth compared to the number of people who surrounded him out of curiosity. This should give us cause for great concern when we look at our churches and observe the few people who are actively taking part in making disciples. Not many of us want to acknowledge the implications of a lack of individual disciple-making efforts, but in Scripture, we see Jesus was well aware of the difficult task he had given his followers.

> And Jesus went throughout all the cities and villages, teaching in their synagogues and proclaiming the gospel of the kingdom and healing every disease and every affliction. When he saw the crowds, he had compassion for them, because they were harassed and helpless, like sheep without a shepherd. Then he said to his disciples, "The harvest is plentiful, but the laborers are few; therefore pray earnestly to the Lord of the harvest to send out laborers into his harvest."
>
> —Matthew 9:35–38

Pray earnestly. Among people who need to embrace their God-given purpose in life to go and make disciples, we need to pray for an uprising of mass proportions. The world has its share of churches, but it seems only a few have embraced the idea of disciple-making. The Kingdom is bigger than the walls surrounding us on Sunday morning. God calls us to go to the ends of the earth with his Gospel, but he also calls us to go to the end of our streets, our hallways, and the other places where we spend most of our time. Go and make disciples and teach them to do the same.

PART FOUR
ISSUES IN DISCIPLE-MAKING

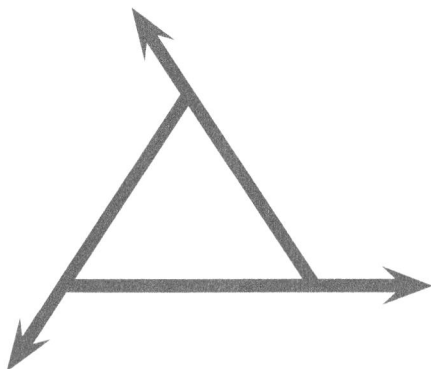

CHAPTER TWELVE

Sharing the Gospel

What Is the Gospel?

The word, *gospel*, simply means "good news." Unfortunately, we have a problem with our understanding of the concept. We whittle it down to the parts of the Bible we think most of the world will find digestible, but the gospel is God's entire story. He created everything, only to see his prized possession rebel and reject him completely. His gracious pursuit of humanity culminated in the death and resurrection of Jesus, and he is continuing to reconcile all things to himself. In his letter to the church at Colossae, Paul eloquently explains the entirety of the Gospel:

> We always thank God, the Father of our Lord Jesus Christ, when we pray for you, since we heard of your faith in Christ Jesus and of the love that you have for all the saints, because of the hope laid up for you in heaven. Of

this, you have heard before in the word of the truth, the gospel, which has come to you, as indeed in the whole world it is bearing fruit and increasing—as it also does among you, since the day you heard it and understood the grace of God in truth, just as you learned it from Epaphras our beloved fellow servant. He is a faithful minister of Christ on your behalf and has made known to us your love in the Spirit.

And so, from the day we heard, we have not ceased to pray for you, asking that you may be filled with the knowledge of his will in all spiritual wisdom and understanding, to walk in a manner worthy of the Lord, fully pleasing to him: bearing fruit in every good work and increasing in the knowledge of God; being strengthened with all power, according to his glorious might, for all endurance and patience with joy; giving thanks to the Father, who has qualified you to share in the inheritance of the saints in light. He has delivered us from the domain of darkness and transferred us to the kingdom of his beloved Son, in whom we have redemption, the forgiveness of sins.

He is the image of the invisible God, the firstborn of all creation. For by him all things were created, in heaven and on earth, visible and invisible, whether thrones or dominions or rulers or authorities—all things were created through him and for him. And he is before all things, and in him all things hold together. And he is the head of the body, the church. He is the beginning, the firstborn from the dead, that in everything he might be preeminent. For in him all the fullness of God was pleased to dwell, and through him to reconcile to himself all things, whether on earth or in heaven, making peace by the blood of his cross.

And you, who once were alienated and hostile in mind, doing evil deeds, he has now reconciled in his body of flesh by his death, in order to present you holy and blameless and above reproach before him, if indeed you continue in the faith, stable and steadfast, not shifting from the hope of the gospel that you heard, which has been proclaimed in all creation under heaven, and of which I, Paul, became a minister.

—Colossians 1:3–23

This is the good news, and it begins with creation. It includes the introduction of sin and our rebellion while showing how God pursued his creation and made a way possible for reconciliation through Jesus. After salvation, there is a continual push for faith, spiritual growth, and Kingdom purpose. The gospel includes the story of creation, fall, rescue, and restoration! Without all of these, it isn't the entirety of the good news we find in Scripture.

This is the gospel: You were created by God, who saved you from yourself, brought you into his Kingdom, and charged you with the mission of making disciples with his Church. Until we fully grasp the entire scope of Scripture, we'll see stories in the Bible as individual narratives, loosely connected by some ethereal notion of the supernatural. In reality, all of Scripture is one big story. It's God's story, and through his love and grace, we get to experience it every day. This is called a metanarrative view of Scripture. Every chapter and verse work together to give a clear, singular picture of God's relationship with his creation.

A Visual Illustration of the Metanarrative of Scripture

If we're going to share the gospel with people, we must train ourselves to share in a way that highlights the entire story found in Scripture. People have used many verbal and visual methods to explain the gospel, all with their own merit. I have settled on a method that I think captures the complete story instead of emphasizing only parts of Scripture. This method is built around the ideas of creation, fall, rescue, and restoration.

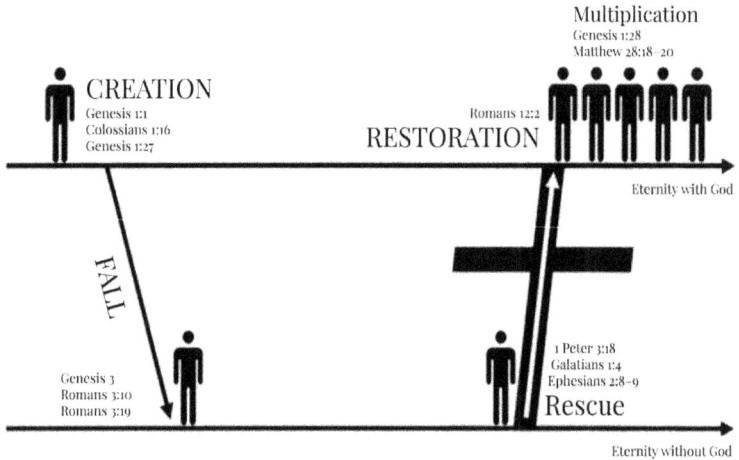

A Metanarrative Explanation

God created everything. Genesis 1:1 reads, "In the beginning, God created the heavens and the earth." In other words, this is his story. In fact, we know through Scripture that everything was created by a Triune God, and it was created for his glory. In Colossians 1:16, we read, "For by him [Jesus] all things were created, in heaven and on earth, visible and invisible, whether thrones or dominions or rulers or authorities—all things were created through him and for him." Everything exists for his glory, and that includes all of humanity. He formed Adam with his own hands, and fashioned man after himself. Genesis 1:27 says, "So God created man in his own image, in the image of God he created him; male and female he created them." We were created to be in perfect fellowship with him forever, living to worship and obey our creator.

Unfortunately, something bad happened. We call it "The Fall." In Genesis 3, we learn that Adam and Eve chose not to trust God, and instead of enjoying a perfect relationship with him, they gave it up. Sin separates us from a perfect God, so instead of being with him forever, Adam and Eve chose a new path, one that led to an eternity without him.

We're born into it because it's so powerful. In Romans 3:10 we find, "None is righteous, no, not one." In other words, we're held accountable for our own sins. One sin is enough to separate us from our Creator forever. Romans 3:19 says, "Now we know that whatever the law says it speaks to those who are under the law, so that every mouth may be stopped, and the whole world may be held accountable to God." Everyone has sinned and deserves God's judgment. Death exists as our punishment for sin; however, there's hope.

God sent his son, Jesus, to rescue us. Being fully God and man, Jesus chose to sacrifice his life on the cross, so we could be forgiven. 1 Peter 3:18 proclaims, "For Christ also suffered once for sins, the righteous for the unrighteous, that he might bring us to God, being put to death in the flesh but made alive in the spirit." Galatians 1:4 speaks of Jesus, "Who gave himself for our sins to deliver us from the present evil age, according to the will of our God and Father." God raised Jesus from the grave and proved his power over death. Those who are drawn by the Holy Spirit and choose to follow Jesus will be forgiven of sin in their past, present, and future.

While we've done nothing to deserve such a gift, God gives it anyway. Ephesians 2:8–9 explains, "For by grace you have been saved through faith. And this is not your own doing; it is the gift of God, not a result of works, so that no one may boast." Jesus's death on the cross made a way for you and me to cross over from death into life.

God is restoring those he has saved. He desires for us to be like Jesus and gives us the Holy Spirit, transforming us from the inside out. Romans 12:2 reads, "Do not be conformed to this world, but be transformed by the renewal of your mind, that by testing you may discern what is the will of God, what is good and acceptable and perfect."

In the beginning, God tells Adam and Eve in Genesis 1:28, "Be fruitful and multiply and fill the earth and subdue it." In a perfect world, God's plan was for Adam and Eve to multiply people who would worship and obey him completely. In Matthew 28:18–20, Jesus reiterates our original purpose of worship and obedience through multiplying disciples. "And Jesus came and said to them, 'All authority in heaven and on earth has been given to me. Go therefore and make disciples of all nations, baptizing them in the name of the Father and of the Son and of the Holy Spirit, teaching them to observe all that I have commanded you. And behold, I am with you always, to the end of the age.'" God saves us through the death and resurrection of Jesus, but his plan for our lives in this world isn't finished. The message is clear: multiply God-worshipers until he comes again. Go and make disciples.

Baptism

Jesus speaks of baptism in the Great Commission, and that automatically means it's a big deal. Therefore, it's important to understand what the Bible says. Scripture speaks about baptism consistently in the New Testament, so there is plenty of information about the ordinance to digest.

What Is Baptism (And Does It Save Me)?

People who believe baptism is necessary for salvation look to one verse as the foundation for their claim.

> For Christ also suffered once for sins, the righteous for the unrighteous, that he might bring us to God, being put to death in the flesh but made alive in the spirit, in which he went and proclaimed to the spirits in prison, because they formerly did not obey, when God's patience waited in the days of Noah, while the ark was being prepared, in which a few, that is, eight persons, were brought safely through water. Baptism, which corresponds to this, now saves you, not as a removal of dirt from the body but as an appeal to God for a good conscience, through the resurrection of Jesus Christ.
>
> —1 Peter 3:18–21

For those who claim this proves baptism is necessary for salvation, I would ask for a deeper and more focused reading. Here, Peter is most definitely talking about baptism, but he is also alluding to the time of Noah. Peter spends the first few sentences establishing the authority of God to save. He then proceeds to make a comparison of the eight people who were saved from the flood and those of us that have been saved by Christ's sacrifice on the cross. There is no denying that Peter says, "And that water is a picture of baptism, which now saves you." If the Scripture were to end there, it would be a strong argument for the necessity of baptism in salvation; however, Peter continues his explanation.

It was as if Peter had already confronted this very idea that we are speaking about right now. What follows is Peter qualifying his own statement. He says, "Not by removing dirt from your body, but as a response to God from a clean conscience. It is effective because of the resurrection of Jesus Christ." In other words, it is Jesus's resurrection that is important. Yes, Peter is using baptism as a representation of our response to Jesus, but our response alone does not save us. In fact, salvation has never been about the power of our response.

> For by grace you have been saved through faith. And this is not your own doing; it is the gift of God, not a result of works, so that no one may boast.
>
> —Ephesians 2:8–9

The Bible paints a clear picture of baptism being an act of righteousness on our part.

> He saved us, not because of works done by us in righteousness, but according to his own mercy, by the washing of regeneration and renewal of the Holy Spirit.
>
> —Titus 3:5

God desires baptism as a testimony and expression of what he has done in our lives, but it is not necessary for salvation. This also seems to be Luke's understanding when he is writing the book of Acts:

> Crispus, the ruler of the synagogue, believed in the Lord, together with his entire household. And many of the Corinthians hearing Paul believed and were baptized.
>
> —Acts 18:8

Note that Luke says that they became believers first, and then they were baptized. We'll return to this idea when dealing with infant baptism. The book of Acts also tells the story of Peter preaching to a group of Jews and Gentiles. In response to the Gentiles becoming believers and receiving the Holy Spirit, Peter asks a very telling question:

Can anyone withhold water for baptizing these people, who have received the Holy Spirit just as we have?

—Acts 10:47

If the Gentiles had already received the Holy Spirit, their salvation was intact. It's ludicrous to expect that God would withdraw his Spirit from their lives if they refused baptism. In fact, baptism was the next logical step *after* salvation.

Because, if you confess with your mouth that Jesus is Lord and believe in your heart that God raised him from the dead, you will be saved. For with the heart one believes and is justified, and with the mouth one confesses and is saved.

—Romans 10:9–10

If baptism is required for salvation, Paul would have made sure to mention it in what is considered his most doctrinally rich letter. Instead, it's not mentioned at all. Baptism is important, but not as an act necessary for salvation.

Infant Baptism

This seems to be a touchy subject when speaking with those (1) who believe in the importance of infant baptism, (2) who have been baptized as an infant, or (3) who have had children baptized as infants.

Obviously, we need to show humility and love in dealing with this situation, but we must ultimately adhere to what Scripture teaches. We have already said baptism isn't necessary for salvation. It is an act of obedience, but it doesn't save us. If we accept this as truth, then the purpose of infant baptism becomes confusing.

I used to travel with a Christian rock band, and one of our stops was in Louisiana. We attended a worship service at a local church where we witnessed an infant baptism. Two things have stuck with me from that experience. First, after the child was baptized, he was paraded around the sanctuary. Every few feet, the minister would lean over and whisper to the congregation, "Through the regeneration of the waters, welcome your new brother in Christ." The other members of the band were young high school and college-aged students. To say they were confused was an understatement. We had a long drive to Georgia and hearing their reactions to the baptism made for an interesting trip.

Second, I remember being transfixed by the father's reaction during the ceremony. There was a look of hope and relief on his face as he wept. It made me realize how accountable we are for what we teach and convey to people. That father believed (or at the least wanted to believe) that his son was saved from death and Hell if anything ever happened to him. No matter what his son did in life or what decisions he made, everything was going to be OK. At that thought, my heart sank in despair, and I began praying that God would draw that young child to himself as he grew older.

There is simply no argument for infant baptism in the Bible. Nowhere can we find one instance of it taking place anywhere in the New Testament. In fact, it's safe to say that baptism only occurred after someone had responded to God's message of forgiveness and repentance. Having said that, please do not assume that the wrath of God is being poured out on you because you were either baptized as an infant or had your child baptized as an infant. God doesn't hate you, and he definitely isn't in the business of punishing you for such a thing.

If you were baptized as an infant but have recently given your life over to God, I would recommend being baptized again. What an awesome testimony to the people around you! If you have had your infant baptized, I would only say this: teach your child to follow in God's ways as he or she grows older. Be the example that they need to see. Nurture your child's interest in the things of God, and when the Holy Spirit speaks to your child, they will have the opportunity to respond. The more you talk about Jesus with your child, the more prepared their heart will be when that time comes. What you teach and experience with your child as they grow is far more important than any ceremony.

Should I Get Baptized?

In short, yes! Not only are we doing what God has commanded, but we're literally following his example. Jesus was baptized out of obedience to his Father. He wasn't seeking forgiveness. Jesus didn't need salvation. Consequently, I would highly recommend baptism as one of the first acts of a new Christian.

Who Baptizes People?

Regarding baptism, there's only one more thing we need to discuss. The Great Commission was meant for all believers, not just pastors in local churches; however, for some reason, the so-called "elite" or ordained Christians get the privilege of baptizing new believers. I see nowhere in Scripture supporting such an idea. I believe if you share the gospel with someone and they choose to respond, it is your privilege to baptize them yourself. Welcome to being a disciple-maker.

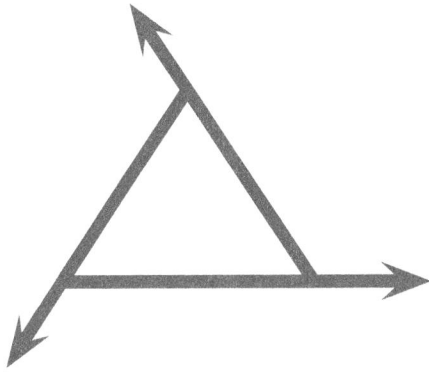

CHAPTER THIRTEEN

The Spiritual Conversation

Angry Christians and Awkward Conversations

As Christians, we've become more concerned with making a stand instead of making a disciple. By trying to force our beliefs on the rest of the world, we've settled for manipulation and a subtle form of tyranny instead of true heart change. In reality, transformation is hard and takes time, but forcing people to accept a shallow form of morality is the quickest way to change things. It's an interesting cycle we've created: our inability to truly influence the morality of others through harsh methods makes us angry, which often pushes us to be more vehement in our desire for moral control, and this pushes people further from the gospel.

Instead of making a consistent effort to bring up Jesus in everyday conversations, we've simply tried to legislate a Christian agenda to little effect. Consequently, we seldom talk about Jesus anymore outside of a church setting, and if we do, it has a minimal impact that makes little difference in the world. Jesus, as a topic, has become taboo because we've refused to talk about him on a normal basis. It's awkward because we've made it awkward. Jesus clearly states how the world will view his followers:

> If the world hates you, know that it has hated me before it hated you. If you were of the world, the world would love you as its own; but because you are not of the world, but I chose you out of the world, therefore the world hates you. Remember the word that I said to you: 'A servant is not greater than his master.' If they persecuted me, they will also persecute you. If they kept my word, they will also keep yours.
>
> —John 15:18–20

We shouldn't be surprised by any ill will that strangers have toward Christians, but we don't even talk about Jesus with our closest allies. It's difficult to talk about Jesus. He stands in opposition to things in which many people partake daily. However, the complicated nature of our culture doesn't excuse us from our responsibility to make disciples, and that requires speaking about Jesus. While the possibility of sharing the Gospel is daunting, believers must start somewhere.

Start with Knowing

Knowledge isn't enough. Growing up, I was taught knowledge was power. Whoever knew the most could benefit the most. In a way, I was taught to guard my knowledge so others wouldn't use it for themselves. The gospel is different. Yes, it has power, but we're not in the business of trying to hoard it for ourselves or use it for financial benefit.

We can't make disciples if we don't know what Scripture tells us about Jesus in the first place. In his letter to the church in Rome, Paul was thrilled at the way they used their knowledge to advance the Kingdom of God.

> I myself am satisfied about you, my brothers, that you yourselves are full of goodness, filled with all knowledge and able to instruct one another.
>
> —Romans 15:14

The Romans used their knowledge of the Gospel to instruct others. For Paul, teaching others the message of Jesus is equated with goodness. We must know the Gospel to fulfill our role as ambassadors of Christ: we can't give away what we don't have.

Engage the World

If we really want to make disciples, most of our efforts will take place in the real world instead of within the confines of our local churches. Most of the time when pastors tell their congregations to go and make disciples, it means they need volunteers to teach small group classes on Sunday mornings (or in homes during the week if they're more "modern"). Small groups are great, but instead of taking the gospel to the ends of the earth, we've settled for trying to make our churches attractive in various ways. We promise community for all and a place to belong, but it's usually at the expense of actually engaging lost people in the world.

Most churches have a hard time getting people who attend on Sundays to even try a small group, let alone commit to one. I've never met a pastor who wasn't overjoyed at having fifty percent of their congregation invested in small groups. Those are "high five" moments in what most would consider healthy churches, but numbers don't always equate to biblical success.

For many believers and pastors, engaging the world usually means throwing a block party or handing out invites to a specific church event, but Jesus had something different in mind when he told us to go and make disciples. In his longest recorded prayer, Jesus specifically asks his Heavenly Father to not take his followers from this world.

> I have given them your word, and the world has hated them because they are not of the world, just as I am not of the world. I do not ask that you take them out of the world, but that you keep them from the evil one. They are not of the world, just as I am not of the world. Sanctify them in the truth; your word is truth. As you sent me into the world, so I have sent them into the world.
>
> —John 17:14–18

Jesus is clear about what he sends his followers to do. He sends them into the world to engage it on a spiritual level with the gospel. The best place for believers to be is right where God has them, but not for the reason we think. We assume the safest place to be is in God's arms. While true from a spiritual and eternal viewpoint, God often calls his children in this physical world to dark and dangerous places. Engaging the world means sharing the gospel and making disciples.

Paul, in his first letter to the Corinthians, addressed the impact of sin, and he encouraged them to flee from it; however, he did not encourage them to flee from their God-given responsibility in this world to make disciples. Running from the people and places where sin reigns would take them away from their responsibility as believers. God places us in the middle of the mess to make disciples.

Paul clarifies the difference between protecting the Body of Christ and running away from sinful people, thereby shirking our responsibility for the Great Commission:

> I wrote to you in my letter not to associate with sexually immoral people—not at all meaning the sexually immoral of this world, or the greedy and swindlers, or idolaters, since then you would need to go out of the world.
>
> —1 Corinthians 5:9–10

We should flee from sin in our own lives, but in making disciples we run toward the people who are caught in its destruction. Jesus called his disciples, trained them, and willingly went to the cross. We are called to live with the same conviction and determination.

The Most Awkward Conversation Ever

Scripture is full of awkward spiritual conversations. From our earthly perspective, Jesus experienced many uncomfortable moments with people when sharing his message. The story of the Samaritan woman at the well is an obvious example.

> Now when Jesus learned that the Pharisees had heard that Jesus was making and baptizing more disciples than John (although Jesus himself did not baptize, only his disciples), he left Judea and departed again for Galilee. And he had to pass through Samaria. So he came to a town of Samaria called Sychar, near the field that Jacob had given to his son Joseph. Jacob's well was there; so Jesus, wearied as he was from his journey, was sitting beside the well. It was about the sixth hour.

A woman from Samaria came to draw water. Jesus said to her, "Give me a drink." (For his disciples had gone away into the city to buy food.) The Samaritan woman said to him, "How is it that you, a Jew, ask for a drink from me, a woman of Samaria?" (For Jews have no dealings with Samaritans.) Jesus answered her, "If you knew the gift of God, and who it is that is saying to you, 'Give me a drink,' you would have asked him, and he would have given you living water." The woman said to him, "Sir, you have nothing to draw water with, and the well is deep. Where do you get that living water? Are you greater than our father Jacob? He gave us the well and drank from it himself, as did his sons and his livestock." Jesus said to her, "Everyone who drinks of this water will be thirsty again, but whoever drinks of the water that I will give him will never be thirsty again. The water that I will give him will become in him a spring of water welling up to eternal life." The woman said to him, "Sir, give me this water, so that I will not be thirsty or have to come here to draw water."

Jesus said to her, "Go, call your husband, and come here." The woman answered him, "I have no husband." Jesus said to her, "You are right in saying, 'I have no husband'; for you have had five husbands, and the one you now have is not your husband. What you have said is true." The woman said to him, "Sir, I perceive that you are a prophet. Our fathers worshiped on this mountain, but you say that in Jerusalem is the place where people ought to worship." Jesus said to her, "Woman, believe me, the hour is coming when neither on this mountain nor in Jerusalem will you worship the Father. You worship what you do not know; we worship what we know, for salvation is from the Jews. But the hour is coming, and is now here, when the true worshipers will worship the Father in spirit and truth, for the Father is seeking such people to worship him. God is spirit, and those who worship him must worship in spirit and truth." The woman said to him, "I know that Messiah is coming (he who is called Christ). When he comes, he will tell us all things." Jesus said to her, "I who speak to you am he."

Just then his disciples came back. They marveled that he was talking with a woman, but no one said, "What do you seek?" or, "Why are you talking with her?" So the woman left her water jar and went away into town and said to the people, "Come, see a man who told me all that I ever did. Can this be the Christ?" They went out of the town and were coming to him.

—John 4:1–30

This passage has all the makings of one of the most awkward conversations in Scripture. First, Jews didn't normally talk to Samaritans who were viewed as dirty, second-class citizens. The simple fact that Jesus made first contact with a Samaritan is surprising. Jews didn't converse with Samaritans if at all possible. It was a racial issue masked as spiritual superiority.

Second, the Samaritan was a woman. Not only did Jewish men tend to avoid Samaritans, but they didn't think very highly of women either. In fact, it was seen as completely inappropriate to speak to a woman in public for some reason. Men didn't even talk to their own wives in public places!

Finally, the Samaritan woman didn't have the best reputation. She was a woman of questionable repute, and that's probably an understatement. She came alone to the well, without any friends or companions. Not only was that dangerous for a woman, but it showed just how out of touch she was with the rest of her people. Women usually came to the well at the same time and enjoyed some interaction with each other. The Samaritan woman had such a bad reputation, no one wanted to hang out with her.

We can learn critical lessons about mastering spiritual conversation if we look at the entire passage. First, the exchange started out with a simple request. Outside of it being an awkward situation, Jesus's question was completely understandable. He was tired and extremely thirsty, and his travel had been long and difficult. In our day and age, we tend to shy away from public discourse with others. Jesus could have waited for his disciples to return before getting water. There was nothing that said he had to talk to the woman, but he made a choice to engage her. The same is true with us as believers. Every conversation we have is a choice to engage this world.

Next, we find Jesus being intentional by directing the conversation toward the gospel. Most Christians today think it's awkward to bring up the gospel in conversation no matter what the initial topic. Jesus knew where he was going with the conversation before it even began. It would help if we were more intentional with our own conversations.

Jesus made the gospel personal. His message spoke directly to the woman at a particular time in her life, and the gospel beautifully relates to all aspects of our lives in the present. In other words, it fits anywhere.

After everything had been said and done, Jesus stuck the landing. We so often try to have spiritual conversations with people, but sometimes we never get to Jesus. If we do happen to make it to the topic of Jesus, we run the risk of it all being in vain if we don't encourage them to take action steps. Jesus told this woman she didn't have to wait to worship. She could do it now! She could choose to follow the Messiah from this day forward if she wanted.

Jesus took an awkward conversation and gave a woman the opportunity to change her life. He listened to her. While everyone else ignored her, the Creator chose to sit down and talk with her. Conversations are important, even uncomfortable ones.

From Spiritual Conversation to Making Disciples

We can talk about Jesus all day long and still fall short of our role as disciple-maker. As simple as it sounds, we must work to get past the conversation and into a relationship. Disciple-making happens during a relationship, but if you're looking to get started, here are some first steps you can take:

Talk about Jesus.

I know it's a simple way to start, but to make disciples you have to talk about Jesus. It might feel awkward or even uncomfortable, but no one said it would be easy. Besides, we need to get to a point where talking about Jesus is a natural thing to do. If you don't talk about Jesus, you won't ever make a disciple.

Pray for people.

One of the easiest ways to bring up Jesus in a conversation is by praying for someone. This is a bit different from *telling* someone you are praying for them because you actually pray for them out loud in the moment. I've had a few people refuse prayer, but most don't. If we listen, people tend to speak of struggles they're currently experiencing. Take those moments to pray and bring Jesus into the conversation.

Invite people to study the Bible with you.

Almost all my disciple-making relationships begin with a simple invitation to study the Bible. While those relationships start with normal conversation, they grow as a result of reading God's Word together. Inviting others to study Scripture is an open door to a deeper relationship, one that may last for an eternity.

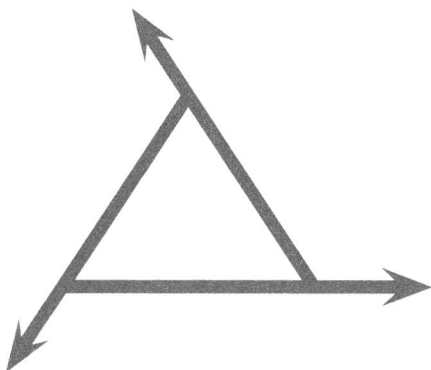

CHAPTER FOURTEEN
The Local Church

As a young student pastor, I knew exactly how to get kids to come to any event. As long as I had food, games, great music, and ample humor throughout the sermon, they would show up. It was truly a "Field of Dreams" mentality: if I would just "build it," they'd come. For the first ten years of full-time ministry work, I did exactly that. I built some of the loudest and liveliest places you could ever imagine. The stunts we pulled were crazy. At one point, I was the only student pastor within a sixty-mile radius that had a worship "mosh pit" every Wednesday night. Looking back, I had the best of intentions, but I'm not sure what most of it did for the Kingdom of God.

I remember being at a local church's Halloween event. I was speaking with the senior pastor and being annoyingly inquisitive as always. I love asking questions and seeing how the minds of others work and putting logical thoughts together. There were thousands of people at this event. By all worldly measures, it was an enormous success. I wish

I would've had a "clicker" to count how many hands my friend shook as he worked the crowd. We got to the edge of the parking lot and there was a huge smile on his face. We turned around and looked over the group of people who had come. Very softly he said, "Jacob, there is different bait for different fish." When I asked him what he meant, he went on to explain that everything they did as a church was to "bait" or attract people so they would come and hear the gospel.

I walked away that evening with a thought I couldn't shake: how many first-time visitors at that event would be back the next Sunday? The older I get, the more I wonder about every event I've ever planned and whether it had an eternal impact. As local churches, we must understand that our success can't be earned or measured by how many people show up to an event or how many people attend on Sunday mornings. If our goal is to get as many people there as possible, then we've missed out on the gospel. The attitude of the church shouldn't be, "Come and see." Instead, it should be, "Go and make disciples."

The local church is one of the most beautiful things we see in the New Testament. When experienced correctly, the impact of gathering with God's chosen people is overwhelming. Paul speaks to the church in Colossae about the Body of Christ in detail.

> Put on then, as God's chosen ones, holy and beloved compassionate hearts, kindness, humility, meekness, and patience, bearing with one another and, if one has a complaint against another, forgiving each other; as the Lord has forgiven you, so you also must forgive. And above all these put on love, which binds everything together in perfect harmony. And let the peace of Christ rule in your hearts, to which indeed you were called in one body. And be thankful. Let the word of Christ dwell

in you richly, teaching and admonishing one another in all wisdom, singing psalms and hymns and spiritual songs, with thankfulness in your hearts to God. And whatever you do, in word or deed, do everything in the name of the Lord Jesus, giving thanks to God the Father through him.

—Colossians 3:12–17

Paul knew that the local church was important. He spent a lot of time planting churches in various areas and training people to lead them. Local churches will always play a part in equipping people to go and make disciples.

We Gather to Experience the Body

Paul knew what it meant to experience the Body of Christ. Remember, his past was mired with hate, arrogance, and the unfathomable murders of innocent Christians. From a worldly perspective, no one in their right mind should have wanted anything to do with him. Simply put, he was a Pharisee who turned on his own people, only to eventually embrace those whom he had spent time persecuting. Paul was the very definition of an outcast, a pariah fit for a lonely existence. Instead, what he found was a true community. In Colossians 3:12–14, Paul echoes the experience of a forgiven man, one who was embraced by people who should have hated him.

"Put on then, as God's chosen ones, holy and beloved compassionate hearts."

Paul's words are for anyone who claims to be a Christian. He tells them to put on "beloved compassionate hearts." When we gather, we experience being in a community with others.

A compassionate heart seeks the benefit of others. If everyone in the Church thought only of themselves, no one's needs would be met, and no disciples would be made. As believers, we must think of others, pushing and pulling them to the betterment of their walk with Christ. We shouldn't gather because of what we get from other people. We gather for the sake of Christ, and for the sake of others.

"Kindness"

Kindness is an extension of compassion. The word Paul uses for kindness portrays a sense of "usefulness." Unfortunately, usefulness is something we have forgotten about in the Body of Christ, relinquishing responsibility to the elite class of Christians who volunteer or actually work at a local church. In contrast, the kindness Paul speaks of demands good works, focusing on what's best for other people. When we extend Christ to others, good works flow from a humble heart, eternally advancing the Kingdom of God.

"Humility"

Humility is the absence of selfish ambition to improve the lives of others. If we're truly called to make disciples, we must think less of ourselves and focus more on loving people. When we seek to serve others instead of ourselves, the mission of Christ takes precedence over everything else.

"Meekness"

Meekness requires that we consider the circumstances and situations of those around us. As believers, we're called to be gentle in our interactions with everyone we meet. Gentleness means we're compassionate in dealing with the mistakes and offenses of others. It's hard to be the church if we're offended by everyone who enters.

"Patience, bearing with one another"

One of the most amazing things we see in the life of Jesus is his patience with the disciples. Quite frankly, the ignorance shown by twelve men is astounding, and Jesus stuck with them every step of the way. Paul understands the patience required for those in the Body of Christ. It took patience and steadfastness for Barnabus to speak up for Paul when no one else in the Church wanted anything to do with him. With patience, we make a promise to walk with others through any circumstance, just like Paul did with the people in Colossae.

"Forgiving each other; as the Lord has forgiven you, so you also must forgive"

There is no place for an unforgiving heart in the Body of Christ. We make too many mistakes to keep up with an ever-growing list of grievances. When we learn to forget and let go of pain, the Church can move forward with healing. Think about it like this: without God making a conscious decision to forgive us, we could not receive salvation. Likewise, without forgiving those who have wronged us (knowingly or unknowingly), we cannot accomplish the mission of the Church.

"And above all these put on love, which binds everything together in perfect harmony"

Paul's proclivity to love is well-documented in his writing. His treatise on love in 1 Corinthians 13 is one of the best-known reflections on the subject, so when he tells the Body of Christ to put on love, we know exactly what he's purporting. Love, as Paul puts it, binds everything together. God's love for us makes it possible for us to love him and other people. When it comes to believers, love is what makes compassion, kindness, humility, meekness, patience, and forgiveness possible in a broken world.

When viewed from a "local church" perspective, all the characteristics we see in Colossians 3 should be evident whenever people gather in the name of Jesus. Too often we're focused on programs and "educating" the masses instead of experiencing the Body of Christ as one, cohesive, purposeful entity. Teaching only works when a dedicated group of people live out God's calling on their lives. Otherwise, we're simply treading water until Jesus returns.

Educating for the Purpose of Education

In my life, God has blessed me with many opportunities to rub shoulders with people through different seasons of employment. One, in particular, has been as a teacher in the realm of public education. Teaching young people is one of the most challenging things I have ever been asked to do, and yet I love interacting with students daily.

As an educator, the main question I hear is, "When am I ever going to use this information?" In other words, the student believes the material to be unimportant. More bluntly, they would rather be doing something different and viewed some of their studies as meaningless and stupid. Unfortunately, sometimes the only answer I had rested on the laurels of my job as an educator: "I teach it because it's in the curriculum." While no administrator ever wants to hear one of their teachers admit to such a thing, it's true. Sometimes, education is simply for the sake of education.

The Church falls into the same trap, but unlike man-made systems of education, the Body of Christ has eternity at stake. Institutions of man will come and go, and none of them will extend beyond this life. The Church's mission is staggeringly different than that of any organization; therefore, education for the sake of education is unacceptable.

I once had a friend who bragged about winning a state "Bible Drill" as a young child. For those unfamiliar with the competition, students compete to see who can find Bible passages the quickest. One evening, my friend frankly admitted he had never read the Bible outside of the passages he had been instructed to find during the game.

If we're not careful, our churches will be filled with people who know a lot about Jesus, but they'll never do anything for the Kingdom of God. Believers will bask in the knowledge of the gospel but never engage in a lost and dying world outside the walls of the local church. If you only go to church to learn more about God, then you have missed what it means to be his child. Knowing Christ is more than knowing about Christ. Paul expressed this in his letter to the church in Philippi:

> But whatever gain I had, I counted as loss for the sake of Christ. Indeed, I count everything as loss because of the surpassing worth of knowing Christ Jesus my Lord. For his sake I have suffered the loss of all things and count them as rubbish, in order that I may gain Christ and be found in him, not having a righteousness of my own that comes from the law, but that which comes through faith in Christ, the righteousness from God that depends on faith—that I may know him and the power of his resurrection, and may share his sufferings, becoming like him in his death, that by

any means possible I may attain the resurrection from the dead.

—Philippians 3:7–11

Paul knew Christ and followed his example. He took on the mission of Jesus and dedicated his life to making disciples. Paul never settled for sitting in a congregation week after week, basking in the light of his own glorious salvation. His story was intricately entwined with our Savior, and it resulted in a life of obedience instead of a life of mere knowledge. When we gather, we don't do so for the education of the masses; instead, we gather for the transforming nature of what it means to take up our cross and follow after Jesus.

We Gather to Worship

Scripture is riddled with story after story of God's people gathering to worship our Creator. There's something about the Body of Christ being together that just makes sense. In our culture, when someone talks about the church, they're usually thinking about a group of people in one place singing and reading the Bible.

Gathering for worship is one of the most amazing experiences of being a Christian, and it's also a glimpse of what praising our Heavenly Father will look like in eternity! Colossians 3:16 emphasizes this aspect of gathering with the body of Christ when Paul writes, "Let the word of Christ dwell in you richly, teaching and admonishing one another in all wisdom, singing psalms and hymns and spiritual songs, with thankfulness in your hearts to God." Gathering for worship is a privilege.

We Gather to Encourage

I remember going to church as a student. I loved meeting with my friends, worshiping, and learning more about God. One of my favorite things was our "night of encouragement." The whole gist of the evening was this: we would each get a paper plate and put our names at the top. For the next thirty minutes or so, we would walk around and write notes of encouragement on the plates. At the end of the evening, we all sat down and read what others wrote. It felt awesome, and I really do cherish those memories; however, my observations as an adult have led me to a frightening conclusion: our encouragement of fellow believers is often shallow, and a bit misguided.

We are the special creation of God, made in his image to reflect his glory (therefore bringing him even more glory). No one in the Body of Christ should ever feel worthless or beneath a certain standing when compared to others. Unfortunately, even in the Church, we've created a dysfunctional "class system," where elite Christians seemingly enjoy the favor of men while others are pitied or despised.

We need to remind people of their unchanging worth in Christ, but what good is that knowledge if believers are not pushed to live as Christ lived? Without the mission of Christ as our end goal, encouragement is nothing more than a glorified form of self-help or motivation. If we're going to encourage and lift up those around us, we must do so with the gospel and mission of Christ at the forefront.

> And let us consider how to stir up one another to love and good works, not neglecting to meet together, as is the habit of some, but encouraging one another, and all the more as you see the Day drawing near.
>
> —Hebrews 10:24–25

I've seen people change (both positively and negatively) under the influence and encouragement of others. It's hard to deny the power of encouragement, and we've been called to use it to bring God glory. The writer of Hebrews encourages the Body of Christ to meet together to encourage one another and push each other toward love and good works. One of the greatest outcomes of consistently meeting with a group of Christians is the incitement to build the Kingdom of God. Good works bring God the most glory.

As believers, we have been called to grow and mature as disciples who make disciples. When we gather to train, equip, and stir each other to love and good works, encouragement takes on a different meaning from that of the world. Gathering with other believers should motivate us to embrace our God-given purpose to advance his Kingdom, not simply make us feel better about ourselves. Our effectiveness in the Kingdom is directly related to our desire and drive for good works.

We Gather to Pray

The purpose of prayer is too great a topic to cover fully in the subsection of a chapter; however, the proclivity to pray is just as important in the modern church as it was in the past. As the Church is birthed in the book of Acts, we see a dependence on corporate prayer as the Body of Christ grows, matures, and advances the Kingdom. Nothing "big" or "great" ever happens in the church unless it is preceded by prayer.

And they devoted themselves to the apostles' teaching and the fellowship, to the breaking of bread and the prayers.

—Acts 2:42

People in the early church prayed together from the very beginning. Prayer was already a big part of the Jewish culture, so it makes sense for it to carry over in importance. God had spent thousands of years engaging with His people, hearing and answering their prayers, and believers expected Him to continue in faithfulness.

When believers pray, it carries a sense of expectation. We aren't praying to God because we're scared that we can't do anything without Him. We *know* we can't do anything without him. We pray because we're convinced that the only way for us to accomplish anything is *through* the power of prayer. God has proven his power over and over again in Scripture, and each time it involves his Church, believers have gathered in prayer. We see such an example in Acts 4 where Peter and John are threatened and released after they have spoken about Jesus before the council.

> When they were released, they went to their friends and reported what the chief priests and the elders had said to them. And when they heard it, they lifted their voices together to God and said, "Sovereign Lord, who made the heaven and the earth and the sea and everything in them, who through the mouth of our father David, your servant, said by the Holy Spirit, 'Why did the Gentiles rage, and the people plot in vain? The kings of the earth set themselves, and the rulers were gathered together, against the Lord and against his Anointed'—for truly in this city were gathered together against your holy servant Jesus, whom you anointed, both Herod and Pontius Pilate, along with the Gentiles and the peoples of Israel, to do whatever your hand and your plan had predestined to take place. And now, Lord, look upon their threats and grant to your servants to continue to speak your word

with all boldness, while you stretch out your hand to
heal, and signs and wonders are performed through the
name of your holy servant Jesus." And when they had
prayed, the place in which they were gathered together
was shaken, and they were all filled with the Holy Spirit
and continued to speak the word of God with boldness.

—Acts 4:23–31

Even in the early life of the Church, prayer played a powerful
role. As believers, we can't sacrifice prayer and obedience and
trade them for our own ideas, goals, pursuits, and assurances.
When we accomplish something without praying first, it is
usually in our own power and on our own merits. For this
reason, we should gather to pray, fortifying our unity of mind
and purpose.

We Gather to Scatter

Finally, we gather as the Body of Christ to train and equip
believers in the mission and methods of Jesus. In other words,
simply coming together isn't enough, it's a means to faithfully
live out God's purpose to go and make disciples. The only way
the Church will ever accomplish God's plan is through the
power of the Holy Spirit and his ability to hold us together in
agreement. Churches play a huge part in preparing believers
to advance the Kingdom of God. In his letter to the church in
Ephesus, Paul writes about the elders' responsibility to send the
Church out fully prepared to do the work of ministry.

And He gave the apostles, the prophets, the evangelists,
the shepherds and teachers, to equip the saints for the
work of ministry, for building up the body of Christ.

—Ephesians 4:11–12

Some people look at this verse and connect "building up the body of Christ" solely with taking care of those inside the church. This type of thinking builds a selfish church, where gathering is the goal and final measurement of success. Scripturally speaking, our call to obedience begins at salvation, is built up and strengthened as we are discipled (inside and outside the church), and is lived out in full view of a lost and dying world. We gather to scatter. We come together to be built up in faith and to be sent out on a mission.

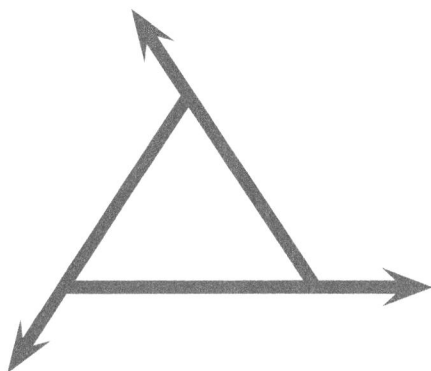

CHAPTER FIFTEEN

The Theory of Convenience

I love my son, Brecken. He is by far the most tenderhearted young man I have ever known, and I get the privilege of being his father. His stature, however, from a worldly standpoint, does not match his demeanor. I stopped growing when I was a sophomore in high school (possibly a freshman), and I top out at a whopping five feet eight when I stand up straight. Brecken has always been one of the tallest kids in his class. There might come a day when he stops growing and everyone passes him up, but for now, he is a giant among men (or children). At ten years old, he passed the five-foot-two mark, and he's seemingly always on the verge of another growth spurt. Having a young son who's constantly growing comes with some interesting side effects.

To put it bluntly, he's always eating. Most of the time, I can't keep the pantry stocked with enough food to satiate his hunger. I remember one day in particular when I noticed every time

I walked through the house, I saw my son eating something. After encountering him in the pantry one time too many, I asked him why he was eating everything in the house. With a confused look on his face, he replied, "Because it's here."

In other words, it was convenient. He didn't have to work for it, pay for it, or prepare it. All Brecken had to do was eat the food, and as long as there was something there to devour, he would continue to do so. Needless to say, I had a fatherly intervention, and we talked about portion control (and a little about economic stewardship).

Brecken was eating because it was convenient, not necessarily because he was hungry (and probably growing at a pace beyond my wildest imagination). The situation reminded me of how we often do the same thing as adults. We'll do what is convenient before we do anything else. Yes, there are always multiple facets of a situation to consider, but most of the time we're searching for whatever makes our lives the easiest, and whatever requires the least amount of work. Unfortunately, this plays havoc in our relationship with God and his calling on our lives.

The Temptation of Convenience

When given more than one option, we will usually take the least objectionable path with the greatest reward. I compare it to shopping for a car. I hate shopping for a car. I feel like everything is working against me, so what I'm looking for is the best deal with the smallest headache. Granted, that's viewing the issue of convenience through a negative lens, but the underlying truth remains. We usually go with whatever is easiest.

In Luke 4, when Satan tempts Jesus, he first appeals to his sense of convenience. Scripture makes it clear that Jesus went into the wilderness with no food or sustenance. Satan clearly knows what drives humanity, and the ease of convenience will always tempt us to walk away from the path God has laid out for us.

> And Jesus, full of the Holy Spirit, returned from the Jordan and was led by the Spirit in the wilderness for forty days, being tempted by the devil. And he ate nothing during those days. And when they were ended, he was hungry. The devil said to him, "If you are the Son of God, command this stone to become bread." And Jesus answered him, "It is written, 'Man shall not live by bread alone.'"
>
> —Luke 4:1–4

Jesus could have easily given in at that moment. He had the power and authority to command the stone to do anything; however, he knew convenience always comes with the risk of receiving what is easy instead of what is right. Unfortunately, this reality can explain our lack of disciple-making.

Disciple-making is difficult. There is nothing easy about laying down your life for others and teaching them to hear and obey Jesus takes time and effort most people aren't willing to give. Making disciples isn't convenient for anyone.

Most of the young men I disciple call, text, or show up at the most inconvenient of times, and they are always apologetic. They'll begin the conversation with, "I'm sorry it's so late," or, "I hope I'm not bothering you." Each time, I express to them there's no need to apologize. Now that doesn't mean I'm not tired when they call, or that it's not inconvenient when they interrupt my family time, dinner time, or time I simply spend in solitude to keep my sanity. It means I'm committed to the work of Christ despite the disruptions.

Jesus took much-needed time to rest, but he also spoke the

truth and invested in the lives of others while tired. In fact, when we see Jesus physically rest, it always follows a time of hard work. He never took the easy way out of anything. Instead, he followed the will of His father no matter what the cost and that included his mission to make disciples while keeping his eye on the cross. His prayer in Gethsemane showed an unbreakable resolve to do what He was sent to accomplish.

> Then he said to them, "My soul is very sorrowful, even to death; remain here, and watch with me." And going a little farther he fell on his face and prayed, saying, "My Father, if it be possible, let this cup pass from me; nevertheless, not as I will, but as you will."
>
> —Matthew 26:38–39

Jesus chose not to contradict the will of his Father. If anything, in great anguish, he proceeded with boldness to the cross. We are tempted to live the most convenient lives possible. If we get the right job, make enough money, and buy the best stuff, our lives on earth will be complete. If we're not careful, we'll begin to imitate the "Rich Man" in Luke 16 who had everything the world had to offer but couldn't take any of it with him in death. Living a convenient life usually builds up treasures you can't keep.

The Point of Disengagement

I remember talking to an older gentleman about disciple-making. He had spent his entire life with one company as an accountant, and God had blessed him greatly. After speaking with him about our purpose to advance the Kingdom of God, he sighed and seemed defeated. He looked at me and said, "That's a young man's game. I've put in my time, and now I'm going to enjoy what life I have left." My heart broke for him at that moment. He knew exactly what God had called him to do, but it was inconvenient for him to give up what he had worked for all those years. Truthfully, he wanted to be left alone; it was the least objectionable option.

We see a similar point of disengagement in Scripture when a young man approaches Jesus. He asks Jesus how to obtain eternal life, but Jesus's answer leaves him sorrowful. What we see is a man unwilling to give up the convenient life he had built.

> Jesus said to him, "If you would be perfect, go, sell what you possess and give to the poor, and you will have treasure in heaven, and come, follow me." When the young man heard this he went away sorrowful, for he had great possessions.
>
> —Matthew 19:21–22

There is a real-world point of disengagement when it comes to following Christ. Everyone must decide whether or not the cost of being a child of God is worth it in the end. Scripture is filled with stories of men and women who wanted a convenient way to follow Jesus. Unfortunately, the convenience of this world will never match the calling of Christ. When people realize that following Jesus means doing what he says and being a part of his mission, they tend to disengage.

> As they were going along the road, someone said to him, "I will follow you wherever you go." And Jesus said to him, "Foxes have holes, and birds of the air have nests, but the Son of Man has nowhere to lay his head." To another he said, "Follow me." But he said, "Lord, let me first go and bury my father." And Jesus said to him, "Leave the dead

to bury their own dead. But as for you, go and proclaim the kingdom of God." Yet another said, "I will follow you, Lord, but let me first say farewell to those at my home." Jesus said to him, "No one who puts his hand to the plow and looks back is fit for the kingdom of God."

—Luke 9:57–62

Jesus was very clear about the requirements for his followers. No one who wanted an easy or comfortable lifestyle stuck around. They either fully embraced the call of Christ, or they walked away disappointed. Sadly, there seems to be another option in our churches today. The third option centers on the idea that we can take on the name of Christ, but somehow shirk from our responsibility for the mission of Christ. We've built our churches in such a way that people can come to church once a week, live a halfway moral lifestyle, and take on the name of Christ, but never do the hard work of becoming a disciple who makes disciples. Sacrificing our lives for the sake of others is too inconvenient.

If we truly want to grasp and take hold of God's purpose for our lives, then our desire for an easy, convenient life must come to an end. Convenience is nothing more than an idol, taking up space and overshadowing the urgency of the gospel. Remember, no one who puts their hand to the plow and gets distracted has the Kingdom of God in mind. Kingdom-minded people are mission-minded people who fully believe in Jesus's command to go and make disciples.

The Desire for Immediate Gratification

My father taught me that it takes time to build something truly great. The older I get, the more I understand what he meant. As a pastor, everything I've ever done that had a quick and immediate effect seemed to fade away over time, but whatever took time to build has, more often than not, remained intact.

Once, I was speaking with a young man I disciple after he had recently graduated from college. We began talking about goals and what he wanted to do with his life, his particular skill set, and the different paths he could take to get there. To say the least, he was ambitious, and I was encouraged to see such focus. His goal was to start his own tech business, help it grow, and then sell it off to focus on missionary endeavors. At first, I was impressed with his business plan and growth projection, but then he started explaining his expected timeline. At the time, this young man was 22 years old, and his plan had him on the mission field, fully funded with the money from selling his company, by the time he was 25. In less than three years, he earnestly and sincerely believed he would have millions of dollars saved up, so he would never have to work again. When I began to push back a little, he became defensive, even to the point of claiming God would make sure it happened. He ended the conversation abruptly and walked away dejected.

We have a problem with immediate gratification. We desire things to go our way, and we want them to happen quickly. Unfortunately, people often quit (or never get started in the first place) if there isn't a sense of satisfaction within a very short time. We'll sacrifice hard work for easy work if it means we experience gratification sooner. In contrast, Scripture tells one coherent story where "waiting" is a key aspect of life.

- Noah built an ark while people laughed, waiting years for vindication and a fulfilled promise from God.

- Abraham waited for a son.

- Jacob waited a long time for a family reunion after rushing into an inheritance.

- Joseph waited a lifetime for vindication and reunion with his family.

- Israel waited for deliverance.

- Israel waited to enter the Promised Land.

- The prophets waited for destruction.

- Israel waited for the Messiah.

- Mary waited for God to fulfill a promise.

- Jesus waited until the time was right to offer himself up as a sacrifice.

- The disciples waited for the Holy Spirit.

- The early church waited in persecution.

- Paul waited for freedom.

- John waited for a revelation.

- We're all waiting for Christ's return.

This list is not exhaustive, but the truth remains evident: immediate gratification is seldom the way God accomplishes his plans. Instead of seeking immediate gratification, we should live in expectation that God is fulfilling what he promised: the restoration of all things. Making disciples is a part of this expectation.

The problem is that making disciples (true disciples) takes time, patience, and dedication. In my experience, most people want an instant "thrill" when it comes to sharing the gospel, and I think this desire helps us understand the conundrum of evangelism/discipleship. In our modern church culture, evangelism and disciple-making are seen as two separate things.

Evangelism is the proclamation of the gospel and discipleship (or disciple-making) is the growth of a believer after they have made the decision to follow Jesus. Sadly, we don't see this distinction in Scripture. Jesus has called us to make disciples, which by the very nature of disciple-making includes the proclamation of the gospel. In other words, if anything, preaching the good news would be a first step in the disciple-making process, not a completely different thing altogether.

Most believers are trained to evangelize up until the point of conversion, but they have no follow-through. Disciple-making requires follow-through. Without follow-through, we are left with confused, frustrated, and disenchanted believers. Oftentimes, most people in this group walk away from Christ due to disillusionment, and it's because of a lack of true disciple-making.

As a young man, I was trained and equipped to share the gospel with clarity, ask for people to respond, and then move on to the next endeavor. I remember one such moment in my life with great clarity. I was in Honduras, preaching and sharing the gospel with students of all ages. One of the schools had one thousand students in attendance on the day I arrived. I remember preaching as passionately as I had ever preached, intricately weaving the gospel story with their own lives, explaining God's love for each of them. At the end of the message, I asked all the students in the crowd who wanted to follow Jesus to respond. Immediately, all the students raised their hands in agreement. I prayed a quick prayer with them (which they gladly repeated), and I was off the stage, in a van, and on to the next school, never to see that group of students again.

I remember basking in the glow of my spiritual accomplishment, somehow thinking heaven was going to have to build a few more city blocks of housing because of what had occurred that day. All my training had led to that moment, and I masterfully soared in the delivery of God's eternal truth.

For some reason, that particular day, God was about to set up a short conversation that would change my life. When we pulled up to the next school, the principal was there to greet us. She asked about our plans, and I explained to her that we wanted to present the gospel and build God's Kingdom. She responded, "Excellent, all of these students have been Christians since birth." At that moment, my heart dropped, and I began a slow descent into despair. I stood in front of the students, preached the gospel (albeit with a little less enthusiasm), and asked them to respond. As I looked up, my despair grew even deeper. Again, every single student was raising their hand in dedication and desire to follow Jesus.

Before I continue, please understand one thing: I am not admonishing those who consider themselves evangelists. I truly believe in the power and beauty of proclaiming the gospel; however, by solely emphasizing the initial proclamation of the gospel, we have abandoned the responsibility of every believer to go and make disciples. Instead, we have taught and trained them to celebrate the immediate gratification of a moment, instead of teaching them to invest in people completely through the process of disciple-making. The convenience of immediate gratification can often distract us from our true purpose in the church, and we're building a body full of people assured of their own salvation because they prayed one prayer at some point in their lives. Scripture warns against such things.

The Sower and the Seeds

While the Holy Spirit is the one who draws people to himself, and Jesus is the one who saves, in his sovereignty, God has chosen all believers and commanded them to be a part of the disciple-making process. In other words, God has ordained for believers to follow through in their proclamation of the gospel. Without such follow-through, the proclamation of the gospel isn't complete, and it can lead to all-too-familiar outcomes. Jesus spoke of these outcomes in Matthew 13.

> "A sower went out to sow. And as he sowed, some seeds fell along the path, and the birds came and devoured them. Other seeds fell on rocky ground, where they did not have much soil, and immediately they sprang up, since they had no depth of soil, but when the sun rose they were scorched. And since they had no root, they withered away. Other seeds fell among thorns, and the thorns grew up and choked them. Other seeds fell on good soil and produced grain, some a hundredfold, some sixty, some thirty. He who has ears, let him hear."
>
> —Matthew 13:3–9

The New Testament makes it apparent that the process of disciple-making should be clearly seen in the lives of all believers. Without disciple-making, people may hear the Word of God and not know what to do next. Remember, disciple-making is an intentional act involving the Holy Spirit, a disciple, and a discipler. While it is the responsibility of the disciple to grow and mature under the direction of the Holy Spirit, Jesus has commanded all of us to take part in this process as a discipler (or disciple-maker).

The Parable of the Sower has three worst-case scenarios that end with the person who hears the truth not becoming a follower of Jesus. Fortunately, through the power of the Holy Spirit, a discipler can be of immense help in any of these situations.

The Seeds Along the Path

> "Hear then the parable of the sower: When anyone hears
> the word of the kingdom and does not understand it, the
> evil one comes and snatches away what has been sown in
> his heart. This is what was sown along the path."
>
> —Matthew 13:18–19

As disciple-makers, it is our responsibility to help those
who don't understand what Scripture is saying. We find one
of the greatest examples of this in Acts 8:26–40. Philip comes
upon an Ethiopian court official who can't understand what he
is reading from the prophet Isaiah, and Philip takes the time
to climb inside his chariot and explain the gospel. Once the
Ethiopian eunuch understands Philip's explanation, he makes
the decision to follow Jesus and be baptized. True disciple-
makers are weapons in such a scenario.

The Seeds on the Rocky Ground

> "As for what was sown on rocky ground, this is the one
> who hears the word and immediately receives it with joy,
> yet he has no root in himself, but endures for a while, and
> when tribulation or persecution arises on account of the
> word, immediately he falls away."
>
> —Matthew 13:20–21

I've seen this happen many times throughout my life.
People will receive the Word of God with joy. The church at
large might even celebrate with them, but time marches on,
convenience takes over, and caring for another person becomes
too burdensome. When this happens, people fall by the wayside
and walk away from faith in Jesus.

As disciple-makers, we are called to walk with people every day, no matter what. If we are consistently sharing our lives with people on a normal basis, then our care for them will only increase during a horrible situation. I disciple a young man named Connor, and there have been numerous times when it would have been easier to simply walk away and let him fend for himself. In fact, there were a few times when it felt like he was making the decision to back away, but I was convicted and continued to pursue him as a disciple-maker. Our relationship actually flourished through that pursuit and became stronger in time. A few years ago, Connor's father passed away from cancer, and it was such a heartbreaking situation; however, Connor was able to persevere and continue his walk with Christ, growing immensely in the following months. I made a promise to Connor to never leave him alone.

The Seeds Among the Thorns

"As for what was sown among thorns, this is the one who hears the word, but the cares of the world and the deceitfulness of riches choke the word, and it proves unfruitful."

—Matthew 13:22

This definitely harkens back to the idea of convenience. As Christ-followers, it is our job to keep those we disciple grounded in the Word of God instead of what our culture throws at them. The "cares of the world" allude to Jesus's previous comments in Matthew 6:19-24 about forsaking the things that don't matter and embracing our "treasures in Heaven." Consistent disciple-making allows for continual reminders of what to focus on and what carries over into eternity. Our discipling relationships and those we have walked with as fellow believers will be treasures that last.

Conclusion

Making disciples isn't convenient. It takes time, effort, and energy. It is emotionally, mentally, and spiritually exhausting, but the disciples we make are Christ's power and legacy working through us and into eternity. We must flee from a life of convenience and seek the purpose for which we were created.

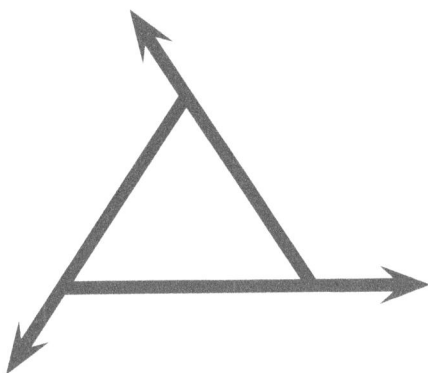

CHAPTER SIXTEEN

The Problem with Belonging

The person who loves their dream of community will destroy community, but the person who loves those around them will create community.

—Dietrich Bonhoeffer, *Life Together*

I love stories. More specifically, I love to tell and be told great stories. I'm a storyteller at heart, and I'm drawn to other peoples' stories. I grew up in a small church in the '80s, and it was always exciting when we had someone show up to give their "testimony," which is obviously a super-Christian way to announce someone's story.

In college, I interned for several churches. I remember one in particular in Robinson, Texas, where I met a student named Jackson whose story was amazing. His father abandoned him at birth, and his mother died when he was only six years old. He was put into the foster system, but a permanent home seemed to elude him for most of his childhood. Finally, a loving family adopted him when he was sixteen. As he gave his testimony in front of the entire youth group, you could physically see his pain as he described his struggle with worth and loneliness. Toward the end of his story, he thanked the church and the students for accepting him into their family as well, and he ended by saying, "Here, I have a place to belong."

I met Nico in Costa Rica. He lived in the middle of nowhere, in a village with a name I can't remember, but I remember his story. I didn't meet Nico in a church or at his home. I met Nico on the street. We were going house-to-house, inviting people into small-group Bible studies being conducted at other houses in their neighborhood. As I passed by Nico, he grabbed my arm and asked what we were doing. After a short introduction, I asked Nico to tell me his story. He didn't have a home, and none of the people in town would let him into their homes, even for Bible study. He then explained that as a young orphan, he had worked his way up in the local street gang. He had established a reputation of fear in the town, and no one would talk to him (which is probably why my friends in the area avoided me while I was speaking with Nico). As we continued our conversation, I could sense some regret when it came to his involvement with the gang. When I asked him what it would take to get out, he responded, "I don't want to leave. I have a place to belong."

As a whole, the feeling of community is one of the most sought-after ideals in all of creation. We need other people to get through life, and we'll search for that sense of belonging no matter what, whether it be positive or negative. Jackson and Nico both found community with very different outcomes. However, even though their communities were different, we must admit that they both found community. If a community is simply the desire to belong to something bigger than yourself, it's not hard to find. As broken individuals, we tend to lay hold of the people, places, or things that lay hold of us. In other words, people find community when they feel accepted, and that level (or feeling) of acceptance differs for each individual. Sometimes we find community and get everything we ever wanted, but other times we only get a sliver of what we want (or think we need) and hold to it as tightly as we can.

From a biblical standpoint, the Christian community is one of the most beautiful things in the world. The love shown to others (especially to those in the Body of Christ), is the telltale sign of who we are as believers. The world will know we belong to Jesus simply because we love each other as Jesus loves us.

> A new commandment I give to you, that you love one another: just as I have loved you, you also are to love one another. By this all people will know that you are my disciples, if you have love for one another.
>
> —John 13:34–35

Jesus loved his followers with sacrificial love, and that's not just a commentary on the cross. Jesus's whole life (including his death and resurrection) was spent as a love letter to his creation. Therein lies the essence of biblical community: It is born out of love, not the other way around. The love of Christ among believers will always grow true community, but the community at face value will never guarantee true love. In its most basic form, this is the problem with what the world (and unfortunately churches) sees as community.

Community As the Goal

We promise people community; however, if *we* don't love like Christ, or if *they* don't love like Christ (or even follow Christ), then it won't be a true community. Whether we want to admit it or not, the rest of the world doesn't have the same priorities as the Body of Christ. Having said that, the community is something people hunger for, but what happens when we promise them something they can get through other local organizations, clubs, or social groups? In other words, we're not the only ones hawking the idea of community. We need to understand that we can give people community without giving them Jesus. It might not be the best of the best, but it's possible, nonetheless. We must be careful with what we're trying to sell to the people in our communities.

What we market matters. In my experience, churches have made a habit of engaging this world with all types of bait to get people in the door. Once inside, that's when they offer you Jesus. If the bait and switch cause people to run for the door, then churches simply pivot to love and hope people stick around long enough to inadvertently fall in love with Jesus.

While driving down a busy street, I saw a progression of signs, each about one hundred feet apart. The first one read, "We have a place for your child." The second sign proclaimed, "We have a place for your student!" As I continued, I found out this magical place also had a place for my college kid, single adults, young married people, and my family, and finally, they had a place for me. One last sign (yes, there was eight total) informed me I would find all these places at the local community church. On the last, larger-than-life sign, was a picture of a purposefully bald pastor with his beautiful wife beckoning me to come be a part of whatever they were doing.

After driving past the signs and almost getting in a wreck straining to see the ads, something struck me. They were marketing to my desire for community. This church had a place for *me*. Sure, I might not have any idea what that place entails or what they believe, but by golly, they had a place for me. They were appealing to my base need for others and betting on the idea that no one wants to be alone forever.

I worked as a student pastor for twenty years, and I can safely say that the "bait" we used to lure students was varied and far-reaching. I have a box of costumes ranging from a regal king clad in purple to a bright yellow, giant banana. There also might be a Chewbacca onesie in there somewhere. I've built backdrops, spent countless hours painting murals, building catapults, and digging two hundred seventy post holes to build a life-sized Pac-Man maze (with people dressed as blue ghosts for good measure). At the end of the day, I couldn't tell you whether or not any of that led to anyone having a deeper relationship with Jesus, but it sure brought the masses.

I remember having a conversation with my father one day. He asked if I had any regrets as a pastor, and I confidently answered, "Yes, plenty." When I expressed how my regrets grew the longer I lived, he simply smiled and said, "Good, that means you're still growing." Today, as I think about that conversation, my mind is filled with regrets, but none more than this: I regret, whether consciously or subconsciously, ever having preyed on a student's loneliness or desire for community simply to boost my numbers at a church.

As Christians (and as churches), it's easy to compromise and twist our actions into something resembling piety, but our motivations are often clear. We can usually make an honest assessment of what we're trying to accomplish by evaluating what we're selling. As a student pastor, I often sold the fun side of things, but I also sold the idea of having something to belong to in this life. I took the loners, outcasts, popular kids, nerds, geeks, artists, musicians, and class clowns and turned them into a family. It was easy. All you had to do was give them a place to belong. Regrettably, I see versions of this in every ministry.

Most of the time, something of this nature isn't as clear-cut as we'd like to think. Often it's hidden behind layers of pomp and circumstance, pushing good things, but ultimately things that can't save anyone. Unfortunately, community is one of those things. It's a great pursuit, unequivocally beautiful in the Body of Christ, but it's not what saves. If we want to build the body of Christ, our aim must be higher than community.

When Jesus called his disciples, he didn't say, "Come be my friend and meet other friends. It's going to be a blast." His initial calling was, "Follow me." As simple as it sounds, it was supremely focused. From the beginning, Jesus made following him the reason to forget everything they knew, leave it all behind, and pursue their true purpose. The invitation to follow Jesus is different than simply finding a place to belong.

"Follow me" isn't a request to join a group or club. It's a call to leave everything behind and pursue only Jesus. It's what the Rich Young Man couldn't do, and I'm often frightened to think how empty our churches would be if "Follow me" was the rallying cry used by ministries today.

In other words, most people who claim to be Christians haven't had to leave much behind. Current roles and responsibilities don't change after becoming a Christian. In their minds, the only thing that changes is their eternal destination (and maybe their morality to a certain extent). But being a follower of Jesus should be much more intentional; therefore, as ambassadors for Christ, we must change our approach. We must put Kingdom before community, and in doing so experience the greatest community that will ever exist.

Kingdom Before Community

We get things backward all the time, but if we pay attention to Scripture, our shortcomings in ministry become frustratingly obvious. Jesus tells his followers to seek the Kingdom above all else. The only pathway to that Kingdom is submission to Jesus and his mission, not community as an end goal. Jesus says, "But seek first the kingdom of God and his righteousness, and all these things will be added to you" (Matthew 6:33).

The only way to experience everything Jesus has for us in this life is to pursue the Kingdom above all else. Pursuing the Kingdom means pursuing Jesus and his mission. It means submission to lifestyle changes and letting go of lifelong dreams to accomplish things of eternal value. Jesus calls all believers to focus on a *single effort*, but the promise of what comes next is where we miss the impact of our steadfast endeavors: if we seek his Kingdom, then "all these things" will be given to us.

Jesus doesn't mean everything we've ever desired will be given to us (praise God for that), but he promises to give us everything we need. If we truly believe that community, as an ideal, is essential to our human existence, then logically the only way to receive and experience true community is through the pursuit of God's Kingdom.

Consequently, if I'm in a discipling relationship, whether as a disciple or the one being discipled, then I should be experiencing quality community. In reality, what I've seen in churches is the desire for community without doing the work of training and equipping people to go and make disciples. If this attitude takes root in a congregation, it is possible to equate success with community rather than the mission of Jesus.

I know this seems like a small discrepancy, but over a long period, these two approaches result in two conflicting outcomes. In one scenario, you have a lot of people who are emotionally satisfied but missionally void of any impact. In the other scenario, where the Kingdom of God is first and foremost, you get a church of passionate ambassadors for Christ, actively building the Kingdom through making disciples. By putting the mission and person of Christ first, we build and strengthen an eternal community.

Outside of my family (whom I serve and disciple), the most intense and satisfying relationships where I experience community are with those I disciple. In other words, as long as I'm making disciples, I should experience the type of community that all humans desire. It's possible to have community without being Kingdom-minded, but it's impossible to truly make disciples and be void of community. Go and make disciples.

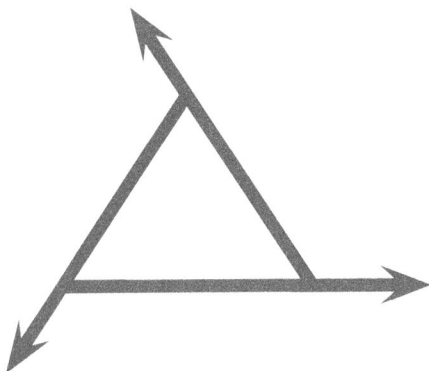

CHAPTER SEVENTEEN

Holiness, Sanctification, and Disciple-Making

Since we have these promises, beloved, let us cleanse ourselves from every defilement of body and spirit, bringing holiness to completion in the fear of God.

—2 Corinthians 7:1

Most Christians I talk to fully believe they have a responsibility to go and make disciples; however, the vast majority of those believers aren't busy making disciples. I remember doing training on disciple-making in the northern United States. Interestingly, the average age of people in the training was definitely above the age of retirement in America. For an entire weekend, we studied, researched, talked about, and practiced what it looked like to go and make disciples. On the final day, a precious follower of Christ came to me in tears. Her name was Margie, and she had been attending church her entire life. It was difficult to hear her as she wept, but her story echoed the stories of countless others I have met. She looked at me and said, "I have spent my entire life following Jesus, but I've never made a disciple."

In moments like the one I spent with Margie, I never had any good, worldly advice, so we simply started praying together. I prayed over her, for her, and for those God had brought into her life, but when she prayed, it was simultaneously excruciating and liberating. At the age of seventy-four, she was pleading for God's forgiveness and begging for more time to make disciples. I began weeping with her. Through her words, I *felt* her pain and anguish, but I also knew that God had changed something inside her. No longer was she content with following Jesus and simply observing the world around her. We spent time praying for people in her life by name, for those she would invite into a discipling relationship. She left with a smile on her face and a renewed sense of purpose.

That same day, I met a man named Lonnie during a break. He stepped up, grabbed my arm, pulled me to the side, and said, "Loving every minute of this, so here's what we do next." Lonnie then proceeded to lay out his plan for the complete discipling efforts in his church, his domain, and in his city. Turns out, he had been making disciples his entire life, and it showed in the way his joy overflowed into every word and sentence he uttered. As he spoke, his passion was almost palpable. When I asked Lonnie where his passion for disciple-making came from, he responded, "I have been set apart for this purpose: to glorify God through making disciples." I turned and looked at the rest of the crowd and asked, "What about the rest of them?" He smiled and answered, "They've been set apart too, just like me. That's what it means to be holy."

Some things tend to keep me awake at night. Most of the

time, it's because I'm praying for my children or worrying about their futures, but there are those times when concepts and deep thoughts cause me to linger in my wakefulness. The matter of holiness is one of those topics, and that night in particular I stayed up, wide awake, and thought about what Lonnie had said.

I'm not sure why I had never meditated on the connection between holiness and disciple-making, but I lay there completely baffled by my own ignorance. Surely, I wasn't the only one who had missed such a fundamental issue as a believer. After all, we've heard from Scripture in thousands of sermons that we are a "holy priesthood," but as many times as we've heard it, there still seems to be a misunderstanding of holiness among God's people.

What Is Holiness?

Holiness in the Old Testament centers on God, his plans, and his people. God is holy because there is no one like him. Hannah's prayer in 1 Samuel 2 is a testament to the holiness of God, showing him as incomparable in every aspect.

> "There is none holy like the Lord:
> for there is none besides you;
> there is no rock like our God.
> Talk no more so very proudly,
> let not arrogance come from your mouth;
> for the Lord is a God of knowledge,
> and by him actions are weighed.
> The bows of the mighty are broken,
> but the feeble bind on strength.
> Those who were full have hired themselves out for bread,
> but those who were hungry have ceased to hunger.

The barren has borne seven,
   but she who has many children is forlorn.
The LORD kills and brings to life;
   he brings down to Sheol and raises up.
The LORD makes poor and makes rich;
   he brings low and he exalts.
He raises up the poor from the dust;
   he lifts the needy from the ash heap
   to make them sit with princes
   and inherit a seat of honor.
For the pillars of the earth are the Lord's,
   and on them he has set the world.

—1 Samuel 2:2–8

For God, holiness means he is high and above all others, both in power and significance. He is perfect, matchless, and unparalleled by anything in his creation. When he says, "I am," it not only means that *he is*, but it also means that *others aren't*.

In reference to his plans, his word, and his people, holiness revolves around the reality that God is using his creation to accomplish his will. God specifically chose the Israelites as his people, paving the way for Jesus and the fulfillment of his plan. The Israelites were set apart as the possession of God for the purpose of his will.

For you are a people holy to the Lord your God. The Lord your God has chosen you to be a people for his treasured possession, out of all the peoples who are on the face of the earth. It was not because you were more in number than any other people that the Lord set his love on you and chose you, for you were the fewest of all peoples, but it is because the Lord loves you and is keeping the oath that he swore to your fathers, that the Lord has brought

you out with a mighty hand and redeemed you from the
house of slavery, from the hand of Pharaoh king of Egypt.

—Deuteronomy 7:6–8

The Holiness of God's people is easy to see when we read
Scripture as one big story. Remember, that's what we call a
metanarrative. Throughout the entire Old Testament, God is
pursuing the Israelites and working out his will to bring Jesus
and salvation through the Jews. They were set apart for this
purpose, and nothing anyone does can change God's eternal
will.

In the New Testament, we see a complete agreement with the
Old Testament when it comes to the holiness of God the Father,
Jesus, and the Spirit. The holiness of God is assumed in almost
every story and letter. Peter even quotes the Old Testament
(Leviticus 11:44) when speaking about our responsibility before
a holy God.

As obedient children, do not be conformed to the
passions of your former ignorance, but as he who called
you is holy, you also be holy in all your conduct, since it
is written, "You shall be holy, for I am holy."

—1 Peter 1:14–16

By the time Jesus was resurrected from the dead, the
holiness of God is undeniably established. There is no one
like him, and his plans are different from those of our earthly
rulers and authorities. Since this is the case, the New Testament
authors focus more on what it means for believers to be holy
and sanctified. I'm not arguing that the New Testament ceases
to speak of God's holiness (the book of Revelation paints a
masterful picture of God's holiness), but the sanctification of
all believers is a beautiful theme throughout. For example, Paul

concerns himself with establishing sanctification as a current reality for anyone whom God has chosen.

> And such were some of you. But you were washed, you were sanctified, you were justified in the name of the Lord Jesus Christ and by the Spirit of our God.
>
> —1 Corinthians 6:11

For Paul, believers were set aside and set apart from the world for a specific purpose. The Church (and therefore those within the Church), acts as God's chosen vehicle for his ministry of reconciliation. Sanctification is a "brand" on all Christians. We are bondservants of Christ due to his sacrifice on the cross. His mission is now our mission, and nothing else matters.

> Or do you not know that your body is a temple of the Holy Spirit within you, whom you have from God? You are not your own, for you were bought with a price. So glorify God in your body.
>
> —1 Corinthians 6:19–20

Whether we fully understand it or not, we are called to a very specific purpose once God saves us and draws us to himself. Sanctification is the mark given by the Holy Spirit for those whom God saves. A full understanding of sanctification is needed to truly grasp our responsibility for making disciples.

Is Sanctification a Process?

First, we must address the idea of sanctification as a process. Most theologians who view sanctification as a process, at least in part, split the idea into two different realities: objective sanctification and subjective sanctification, which are seen as two parts of a whole. Objective sanctification refers to the finished work of Christ; it is completed, lacking nothing in power, purpose, or effect. Subjective sanctification indicates the idea of Christ's completed work being progressively realized as believers grow and become more like Christ.

At first glance, this understanding seems to fit within the confines of Scripture and historical doctrine. However, when looked at from a metanarrative standpoint, I'm not sure it holds up. At the very least, we need to acknowledge some possible slippery slopes if we adhere to this "duality" in sanctification. While it's nothing that should cause disfellowship among believers, it does have an impact on the way we view our responsibility to make disciples.

At least eighteen times in Scripture, multiple authors use the term for sanctification in reference to all believers. Fourteen of these biblical references are describing a *completed* act of God. No major commentaries or modern theologians disagree with this fact.

In the Gospel of John, Jesus is offering a prayer for all believers. John 17:17 is in keeping with an understanding of a completed act. In this instance, we are either in truth or outside truth. There is only one truth, and we cannot progress into truth. We are either enveloped by truth, or we aren't. Truth will always be truth, and there is never a progressive understanding of truth. Yes, we will grow as Christians and learn to live in truth, but that is not an issue of sanctification. Remember, sanctification is an issue of being set apart for a purpose, not necessarily *living* in that purpose at the moment. Whether I'm currently living in obedience or not has nothing to do with God's declaration of my holiness for his purposes. Verse nineteen of John 17 is simply a continuation of this reality. As followers of Christ, we are set apart from others by the truth of God.

Sanctify them in the truth; your word is truth. As you sent me into the world, so I have sent them into the world. And for their sake I consecrate myself, that they also may be **sanctified** in truth.

—John 17:17–19 (emphasis added)

Luke's understanding of sanctification was clear. For him, sanctification was not a progressive matter. God sets apart all people he has forgiven and saved through faith. They are different in function, purpose, and standing from the rest of creation.

And now I commend you to God and to the word of his grace, which is able to build you up and to give you the inheritance among all those who are **sanctified.**

—Acts 20:32 (emphasis added)

But rise and stand upon your feet, for I have appeared to you for this purpose, to appoint you as a servant and witness to the things in which you have seen me and to those in which I will appear to you, delivering you from your people and from the Gentiles—to whom I am sending you to open their eyes, so that they may turn from darkness to light and from the power of Satan to God, that they may receive forgiveness of sins and a place among those who are **sanctified** by faith in me.

—Acts 26:16–18 (emphasis added)

In his first letter to the church in Corinth, Paul's grasp of sanctification is firmly on display. The issue of being set apart is a work God has completed for all those who are a part of the

Body of Christ. First Corinthians 1:30 equates sanctification with being *in Christ Jesus*; this should be understood as a full adoption into Jesus instead of a slow and steady process. First Corinthians 1:2 and 6:11 are clear about the sanctification of all believers, having changed in "position" before Christ, now being set apart for his mission and purpose.

> To the church of God that is in Corinth, to those **sanctified** in Christ Jesus, called to be saints together with all those who in every place call upon the name of our Lord Jesus Christ, both their Lord and ours.
>
> —1 Corinthians 1:2 (emphasis added)

> And because of him you are in Christ Jesus, who became to us wisdom from God, righteousness and **sanctification** and redemption.
>
> —1 Corinthians 1:30 (emphasis added)

> And such were some of you. But you were washed, you were **sanctified**, you were justified in the name of the Lord Jesus Christ and by the Spirit of our God.
>
> —1 Corinthians 6:11 (emphasis added)

Paul's letters to the church in Thessalonica also take on the same view of sanctification. God did not sanctify us completely so that we would live *some* of our life for him and keep the rest for ourselves. He desires that we fully live in his sanctification.

> For this is the will of God, your sanctification: that you abstain from sexual immorality.
>
> —1 Thessalonians 4:3

But we ought always to give thanks to God for you, brothers beloved by the Lord, because God chose you as the firstfruits to be saved, through **sanctification** by the Spirit and belief in the truth.

—2 Thessalonians 2:13 (emphasis added)

According to Paul, sanctification and salvation are incapable of being separated unless we are willing to accept the idea of progressive salvation; however, we were sanctified when we were saved. If sanctification has so much to do with God's calling on our lives, why would we ever think of it as progressive? Are we more called *now* than we were yesterday? Are we more set apart for God than when we first began our relationship with him?

The writer of Hebrews seems to distance himself from the idea of progressive sanctification.

For he who **sanctifies** and those who are **sanctified** all have one source.

—Hebrews 2:11 (emphasis added)

And by that will we have been **sanctified** through the offering of the body of Jesus Christ once for all.

—Hebrews 10:10 (emphasis added)

How much worse punishment, do you think, will be deserved by the one who has trampled underfoot the Son of God, and has profaned the blood of the covenant by which he was **sanctified**, and has outraged the Spirit of grace?

—Hebrews 10:29 (emphasis added)

In Hebrews 2:11 the writer firmly establishes that God sanctifies us, but in the same sentence, he also clearly argues for *full* sanctification. All those in Christ are sanctified. Hebrews 10:10 and 10:29 also seem extremely adamant about sanctification being a fully realized standing before God and all of creation.

Finally, in his first letter, Peter addresses the "elect." Here, believers are in Christ because they have been sanctified by the Spirit. Members of the Body are currently living *in* that sanctification.

> Peter, an apostle of Jesus Christ, to those who are elect exiles of the Dispersion in Pontus, Galatia, Cappadocia, Asia, and Bithynia, according to the foreknowledge of God the Father, in the **sanctification** of the Spirit, for obedience to Jesus Christ and for sprinkling with his blood: May grace and peace be multiplied to you.
>
> —1 Peter 1:1–2 (emphasis added)

At the very least, surely, we can all agree that everyone in the Body of Christ has been set apart by God for his mission and purpose. Scripture teaches that sanctification is a fully understood and realized position; however, let's take a look at some of the verses people tend to quote when they're viewing sanctification as a process.

Difficult Passages on Sanctification

While I despise referring to any Scripture as "difficult," there are three instances in particular when taken by themselves, that would seem to imply a form of subjective sanctification. We will look at each individually, but we must remember our God is not prone to confusion or contradiction.

I am speaking in human terms, because of your natural limitations. For just as you once presented your members as slaves to impurity and to lawlessness leading to more lawlessness, so now present your members as slaves to righteousness leading to **sanctification**. For when you were slaves of sin, you were free in regard to righteousness. But what fruit were you getting at that time from the things of which you are now ashamed? For the end of those things is death. But now that you have been set free from sin and have become slaves of God, the fruit you get leads to **sanctification** and its end, eternal life.

—Romans 6:19–22 (emphasis added)

It is important to know and understand the main idea of the above passage. Paul is describing a dichotomy that exists between people separated from Christ and people joined with Christ, encouraging those who are in Christ to be slaves to righteousness. In other words, Paul isn't arguing for progressive sanctification, but for all believers to live as righteous people who have been sanctified. When we live as Jesus lived, only then will people in this world see us as the "set apart" Body of Christ we already are. In other words, Paul is pleading with Christians to embrace and live in the reality of God's holiness instead of simply acknowledging it exists in Scripture.

Now may the God of peace himself **sanctify** you completely, and may your whole spirit and soul and body be kept blameless at the coming of our Lord Jesus Christ.

—1 Thessalonians 5:23 (emphasis added)

If 1 Thessalonians 5:23 is taken by itself, Paul seems to be offering a progressive view of sanctification here; however, we must remember that Paul already addressed the issue of sanctification in chapter four of the same letter. Taking our previous understanding and knowledge of that passage, it makes more sense to view the Spirit's work of sanctification as final and complete, while allowing him to change us in such a way as to fully live in that sanctification. In this way, God's fully sanctifying us, and our fully living in that sanctification are two different things.

Ask yourself this question: As Christians, do we already stand blameless before God because of the finished work of Christ, or do we somehow earn the title of blameless by learning and growing? Scripture teaches we are already declared blameless, but our current actions may not match God's declaration. In an astonishing mystery of the gospel, we already are what we don't currently act like, but this is only due to the miraculous work of Jesus Christ.

> And you, who once were alienated and hostile in mind, doing evil deeds, he has now reconciled in his body of flesh by his death, in order to present you holy and blameless and above reproach before him, if indeed you continue in the faith, stable and steadfast, not shifting from the hope of the gospel that you heard, which has been proclaimed in all creation under heaven, and of which I, Paul, became a minister.
>
> —Colossians 1:21–23

If I can do nothing to reconcile myself before God, then it's impossible to stand blameless before him while relying on my strength. If Jesus has saved me, then I already stand blameless before the Father. That is, what I'm currently doing doesn't necessarily match who I am. Paul struggled with this exact situation.

> So I find it to be a law that when I want to do right, evil lies close at hand. For I delight in the law of God, in my inner being, but I see in my members another law waging war against the law of my mind and making me captive to the law of sin that dwells in my members. Wretched man that I am! Who will deliver me from this body of death? Thanks be to God through Jesus Christ our Lord! So then, I myself serve the law of God with my mind, but with my flesh I serve the law of sin.
>
> —Romans 7:21–25

Hallelujah! Who I am isn't determined by what I've done once reconciled to God. Yes, I still struggle with the actuality of sin, but my standing before God can never be retroactively adjusted to reflect my previously sinful state. The blood of Christ has washed every sin away, and if God has cleansed me, he has also set me apart for a purpose. Let's take a look at one last verse on sanctification: "For by a single offering he has perfected for all time those who are being sanctified" (Hebrews 10:14).

By far, this is the most debated verse in the Bible dealing with sanctification. At the heart of the debate is the use of the present passive participle of *sanctification*. In Greek, the present participle may be understood progressively, repetitively, or as timeless. Many scholars read this verse with a progressive understanding of sanctification but given the preponderance of evidence seen in Scripture, it makes more sense to view it as timeless, an interpretation favored by translations like the *New American Standard Bible*, and the *Holman Christian Standard Bible*.

Since the focus of the passage surrounding Hebrews 10:14 is fixed on the idea of Jesus's completed work of salvation, it makes sense to read this verse as a completed act as well. Otherwise, the main focus of the author is diluted. In his commentary on the book of Hebrews, F. F. Bruce explains the everlasting nature of sanctification:

> In v. 10 the emphasis lay on the unrepeatable nature of the death of Christ as the sacrifice by which his people have been set apart for the worship and service of God; here their character as the people thus set apart is simply indicated in timeless terms, because emphasis is being laid on the fact that by that same sacrifice those who have been cleansed and "perfected" are now eternally constituted God's holy people.[5]

When viewed through the entire lens of Scripture, the immediacy and permanence of sanctification are clear. The Word of God does not separate sanctification into two groups, and this nullifies our need to do so. Have we been sanctified? Yes. Is God sanctifying us still? I would argue that this idea does not match the metanarrative we see in Scripture. In other words, because of the supernatural aspect of God's character and will, my sanctification is complete, but my growth is ongoing; however, growth is not the same as sanctification. There is no scriptural precedent for separating sanctification into two different realities. Sanctification is one inseparable truth. We have been set apart by God for his purpose and pleasure.

---

5   F. F. Bruce, *The Epistle to the Hebrews* in *The New International Commentary on the New Testament*, rev. ed. (Grand Rapids, MI: Wm. B. Eerdmans Publishing Co., 1990), 247.

Sanctification and spiritual growth are two different things; however, both are acts of the Spirit. Sanctification is a declaration of salvation. God sets apart his chosen people for his mission. While spiritual growth is most definitely a progressive aspect of our relationship with Jesus, sanctification is not. If God declared me holy at the moment of my salvation, I am no more holy or set apart now than I was when I began walking with Jesus. In contrast, due to the work of the Spirit, I now look, think, act, and speak more like Jesus than when I first started my journey as a believer. That is growth.

Our understanding of sanctification must rely on what happened first. In this case, God sanctified us when he saved us. If we truly are a sanctified people no matter what we do, then at the very least, we should understand that our inability to live up to that ideal does not disqualify us from striving for it with our entire being.

Sanctification is not perfection. I am not perfect, and I will never be perfect in this life. Sanctification has nothing to do with my ability to get anything right. It has everything to do with God's calling on my life and what he requires of his children. God's desires for me are matchless, but I am not.

As I grow in my own Christlikeness, I begin to match the holiness of his call on my life, but whether I am at the beginning of my relationship with Jesus or near the end of my life on earth, I am no more set apart for God's purpose than when he first began his work in me. Sanctification is not a process, but as we grow in Christlikeness, we begin to live more and more in the reality of our declared holiness.

Sanctification and Disciple-Making

Our understanding of sanctification has major implications for disciple-making. Unlike sanctification, disciple-making is a process. Remember our compass illustration? Disciple-making is reorienting our life compass back to true north, or back to the image of God in which we were created. As disciples, we allow the Holy Spirit to work in our lives in such a way that we grow in our ability to imitate the heart and mission of Jesus.

The Bible is clear that every believer carries with them the responsibility for disciple-making. Jesus commands us to go and make disciples. On this earth, disciple-making is our purpose. It is how we glorify God the most, acting in obedience.

We have been set apart to glorify God through going and making disciples; however, to this day, the majority of questions I get from believers are from those still struggling with finding their reason for living. When asked about their purpose, most Christians can muster some answer, often about glorifying God (which is absolutely true), but the "how" alludes them. They'll mention loving others and having good morals, but rarely will they ever land on disciple-making. Whether it's too hard, time-consuming, or inconvenient, we don't want to measure how we glorify God through making disciples, and the reason is clear: most of us don't follow that commandment. We'd rather equate our worship to attending a church or being morally superior in some way to our fellow man. If we measured our worship through how we are reconciling this world back to God through making disciples, most of us would fail miserably.

When conversing with fellow believers about our lack of disciple-making, I often turn the conversation inward and ask about their efforts in building the Kingdom of God. Most of the time, people respond with, "I'm just not there yet," or, "I don't have the gifts to do that," but that mentality contrasts with the biblical view of sanctification.

Sanctification makes our standing before God very clear: we either obey God in his command to go and make disciples, or we live in disobedience. In other words, our lack of readiness or motivation to follow through doesn't matter. From the moment you are saved and sanctified, you have the responsibility for disciple-making. There is never a season of life (whether immature or mature) when the Great Commission is placed to the side in order for us to focus on our own efforts.

When we view sanctification as a process, there's always the potential for us to think we haven't progressed enough in our calling to do the work of the Church. We tend to think that only so-called elite Christians are capable and able to fulfill their purpose. The rest of us simply exist, delaying our purpose and settling into a sad version of life: in this version, the workers aren't concerned about the harvest. They're only interested in gleaning enough produce for their own sustenance.

Sanctification is not an issue of becoming *more* holy, but we should grow and mature into faithful disciples. If we could be "more holy," that would mean Jesus's command to go and make disciples doesn't apply to every believer at every point in their walk with Christ. This misunderstanding is the main hindrance to the Church in dealing with the Great Commission. We've either convinced ourselves that we're not "Christian" enough to go and make disciples, or we lazily claim we're not ready; that is, we're either scared or ambivalent, and that's not the life God wants for any of his children. You have already been sanctified and set apart, now go and make disciples.

References

Bartholomew, Craig G., and Michael W. Goheen. *The Drama of Scripture: Finding Our Place in the Biblical Story*. Grand Rapids, MI: Baker Academic, 2014.

Bruce, F. F. *The Epistle to the Hebrews* in *The New International Commentary on the New Testament*, rev. ed. Grand Rapids, MI: Wm. B. Eerdmans Publishing Co., 1990.

Clem, Bill. *Disciple: Getting Your Identity from Jesus*. Wheaton, IL: Crossway, 2011.

Liederbach, Mark, and Seth Bible. *True North: Christ, the Gospel, and Creation Care*. Nashville, TN: B & H Academic, 2012.

Sailhamer, John H. "Genesis" in *The Expositor's Bible Commentary*, ed. Frank E. Gaebelein. Grand Rapids, MI: Zondervan, 1990.

www.ingramcontent.com/pod-product-compliance
Lightning Source LLC
Chambersburg PA
CBHW071839090426
42737CB00031B/1611